Making an impact online . . . on a Shoestring

Creating a website that really works without breaking the bank

Antóin Ó Lachtnáin

BLOOMSBURY

First published in Great Britain in 2007 by A & C Black Publishers Ltd

This edition published 2011
Bloomsbury Publishing Plc
50 Bedford Square, London WC1B 3DP

A CIP record for this book is available from the British Library.

ISBN: 978-1-4081-3990-5

This book is produced using paper that is made from wood grown in managed, sustainable forests. It is natural, renewable and recyclable. The logging and manufacturing processes conform to the environmental regulations of the country of origin.

Design by Fiona Pike, Pike Design, Winchester

Typeset by RefineCatch Limited, Bungay, Suffolk

Printed and bound by CPI Group (UK) Ltd, Croydon, CR0 4YY

CONTENTS

INTRODUCTION

How is the Internet affecting your business? Even if you don't use it yourself, your customers and suppliers already are. Buying and selling online is an everyday activity for many consumers. Some of your suppliers are probably selling online and may be trying to find ways to reach the end-customer directly. As a result, they may be able to sideline or bypass smaller businesses such as yours.

Don't sit idly by and watch this happen! Big opportunities await small businesses on the Internet and there are many ways you can make your company more efficient and attractive for your existing customers by providing even basic services to them online. There are also opportunities for growth. Although the media give all the attention to multi-million dollar Internet deals, there are many successful small and one-person businesses trading successfully online, and sites like eBay and Google provide access to a global marketplace for all businesses. If you can provide a distinctive product or service that people want, there is no reason why the Internet cannot help you build a successful small company.

So how do you get started? That's where this book comes in. It will help you get the basics in place, including the right domain name, a good broadband connection, an e-mail set-up and a social media presence with the likes of Facebook. It guides you through the process of setting up a basic website that will meet your business needs, and explains how to sell goods and receive payments off it, if that's appropriate to you. It also explains the basic principles of Internet marketing and gives you straightforward, practical strategies that will get the word out about your business and bring traffic to your website.

Making do on a shoestring budget is an issue for any small business trying to get online: you may not be in a position to invest money in something that isn't going to generate income right away. The good news is that many of the strategies in the book can be implemented without spending a fortune, and some can even save you money in the short term (by reducing your use of the phone and fax, for example). When splashing out is unavoidable, this book suggests ways in which you can use your cash as effectively as possible. There are also warnings about some of the pitfalls related to budget-watching: not every potential cost saving is worthwhile, especially if there's a risk that it could cause serious disruption later on.

Most importantly, this book will help you to think strategically about doing business online. The Internet is changing business profoundly: customers have more choice and distance is less of a barrier than ever before. How do you make your business stand out in this new world? Each chapter will present examples of websites that demonstrate how companies large and small have tapped into the power of the Net to create better customer relationships or to make their businesses more efficient.

Your shoestring budget shouldn't be a barrier to getting on the Internet. As long as you have good ideas and follow the steps, you'll have no trouble making an impact online.

1 CREATING AN EFFECTIVE INTERNET STRATEGY

The Internet has revolutionised the way many businesses operate, and while it has hampered some small businesses, it's helping many others to grow. So how can you make the Internet work for your business, without spending a lot of money? The first thing is to think 'strategically'.

'Strategy' is a broad topic, but the most important thing to do when devising a business strategy is to step back from your business and look at it in a new way.

For example, Jeff Bezos, founder of the Internet mail-order company Amazon.com realised that the most important part of a bookshop business was not the actual stock and the shop premises but the information supplied about the books. He concluded that if this information were cleverly presented, it could provide a valuable service to book purchasers. As a result of this thought process, Amazon is now by far the biggest book retailer in the world and has a strong presence in many other retail areas too.

Similarly, when Pierre Omidyar started up eBay, he recognised that having physical premises was not essential to running an auction house for second-hand goods. He built an auction house on the Internet, so that sellers and buyers could list goods and make bids from their home or office. As a result, his costs were much lower than those of a conventional auction house and he could quickly scale his business to handle hundreds of thousands of sales. Today, eBay handles more auctions than anybody and the business has expanded to take in classified ads, local advertising and electronic payments.

In the UK, Tesco took its retail business and, using a relatively simple website, made it possible for customers to order online. Many of their online grocery counterparts invested heavily in developing special warehouse facilities to handle online sales. Tesco chose to do things in a cheaper, simpler way. It used its existing stores as depots and employed its existing staff to do the packing. As a result, its investment was relatively small and the venture was able to become profitable within a short time. Of course, this was only possible because Tesco was such a well-known brand and already had some of the IT (information technology) systems it needed in place. This strategy has helped Tesco become the third-biggest online retailer in the UK.

Directski.com, a small web-based winter sports tour operator which began operating in the Irish marketplace, has established a substantial business selling ski holidays to the British, US and European markets. Customers can now book their flights and package holidays less expensively through its Internet website.

At the same time, small local travel agents of a similar size to Directski.com have gone to the wall as a result of the Internet revolution. Companies such as Directski.com can survive, in spite of their small size, by focusing on a niche and providing a level of customer service that is not available from the big players.

CREATING AN EFFECTIVE INTERNET STRATEGY

Thousands of small businesses have established themselves on eBay, selling an amazing variety of second-hand goods. eBay knows it has to compete quite openly on reputation and service, and its simple structure and low overheads allow it to do this.

How did these companies make the leap to become thriving businesses that took advantage of the Internet? They looked at a

Directski.com has built an international business in the ski holiday business. All sales are conducted through its website or by telephone from the company's base in Dublin.

traditional business, and they recognised how the opportunities that the Internet brought could transform their industries.

How the Internet is affecting business

The Internet is changing the way that buyers purchase and consume goods and services.

New information sources

Before the arrival of the Internet, information about products and services was hard for customers to come by. Leaflets and brochures were distributed by local agents, and resellers acted as powerful information brokers who controlled the supply of datasheets and product information. There were relatively few opportunities for

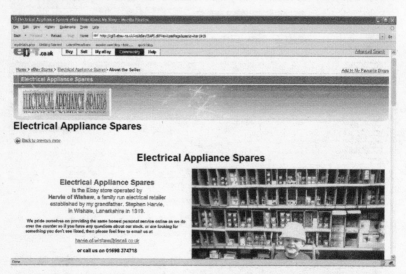

An established family business is using eBay as an extra channel to market its electrical goods to the public. By doing so, it increases its profile and gains access to an audience that would otherwise be inaccessible.

customers to meet sellers, and sales calls and trade shows were the main occasions when information could be obtained easily. The customers for a particular product rarely had the opportunity to communicate with each other except in circumstances dictated by the sellers.

Detailed information about almost any product is now available to download from manufacturers' websites. By visiting Web forums or joining mailing lists, you can even get relevant advice from people in the same industry or facing the same challenges as you, even if they are thousands of miles away. Equally, you may be able to find a seller in another country who can give you a better price on the

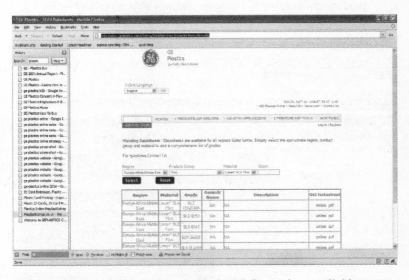

The GE Plastics website makes technical information available to any Internet user, anywhere in the world. Previously, this information would only have been available in print form to specialists who had access to GE sales personnel and through distributors.

same or a similar item. If you have larger-scale needs, you may even be able to find a manufacturer who will be prepared to make you what you want, to your exact specifications.

> Type 'custom manufacturing' into a search engine, such as Google, to get an idea of the manufacturing facilities that modern businesses can potentially access.

The changes brought by the Internet are even more telling in the service industries. Previously, a travel agent was the only source for up-to-date schedule and fare information on air travel available to consumers. As a result, customers inevitably ended up booking through a travel agent, who sometimes retained as much as 5 or 10 percent of the ticket's value as commission. The airlines quietly accepted the travel agents' power, because these agents were the only people who could give them access to their markets.

Nowadays, the very same information about routes, fares and availability of flights can be obtained through many different websites, as well as from the airlines themselves. Airlines no longer need the agents to sell their tickets, and so are comfortable bypassing them and refusing to pay any commission. Customers can book directly with an airline for the cheapest price. You can still go through an intermediary like a travel agent, but you will generally have to pay extra for the convenience.

But while old 'intermediary' businesses such as the local travel agent have been severely damaged by the Internet, new intermediary businesses are sprouting up. In the travel sphere, sites like Expedia and

Orbitz.com can succeed by offering you the fastest or most economic route for a particular trip. There are still commissions for intermediaries to be had from hotels and car rental companies, and these companies often charge slightly more than the airline's own website.

Even businesses such as the local doctor or medical centre are finding themselves under pressure from the Internet. Patients often consult online health sites before visiting their GP, and they go to the surgery with information and views about their illness. They can find out about alternative treatments for their medical problems and can even get in touch with experts in other countries.

Many other types of 'intermediary' business are being hit by these changes. For example, the bookshop is traditionally the intermediary between the publisher and the reader. Before the Internet, information about books was generally accessed via such stores, and most books could only be bought or ordered in these retail outlets. Firstly, the Internet made information about books more widely available. Having access to details about books that were not easily obtainable in the stores made people want to purchase these books. Secondly, the Internet made it possible for customers to order books from online stores such as Amazon.com, which in turn uses online database to access items that it doesn't have in stock. Goods are only ordered from publishers as customers require them.

Book retailing has been hit sooner and harder by these changes than many other sectors, because the nature of its business is well suited to the Internet. Customers may not be able to get the same or equivalent book from local suppliers and so are prepared to go online; the cost of the item is relatively low, and so conservative shoppers are willing to try something new. The product can be easily shipped and has an international market. Amazon.com has done a great job at utilising the Internet to convey detailed information about books to guide shoppers to the right book and then help them make a purchasing decision. Amazon.com has used its early lead as a seller of traditional physical books and goods to position itself in the totally new business of eBooks that is now emerging. Using the Kindle handheld device, books can be sent to readers in electronic format. As the Kindle devices become more widespread, this will once again change the way readers buy books.

However, these changes are now impacting on other sectors in the same profound way, albeit sometimes at a slower pace. Shoppers can find alternative outlets for almost any product through Internet search engines or through the online auction site eBay.

It's also easier for prospective customers to deal with distributors in other countries or deal directly with manufacturers. Sites such as **Alibaba.com** (now owned by Yahoo) allow sellers and even end-customers in the western world to get in touch with manufacturers in the Far East with a minimum of fuss and hassle.

As a result, intermediaries in all sectors have to work harder to earn their margins. They have to provide a clear definable benefit to the customer in order to stay in business. Otherwise, the customer will find a way to bypass the intermediary and work directly with the manufacturer of the product.

The changes have also had an effect on the people who make the products. Although there is an opportunity to enter new markets, there is ever-increasing pressure from existing customers for companies to be responsive to new needs, as well as to improve product quality and reduce prices. It's difficult for Western companies to compete on price alone; they have to find new ways to differentiate themselves.

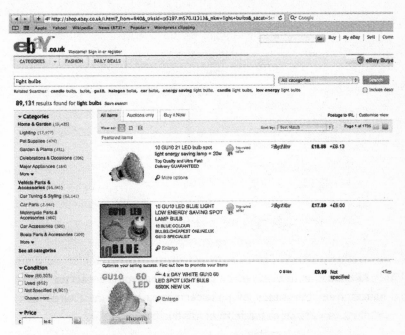

The results of a search for 'light bulbs' on the eBay site. Consumers can find and buy almost anything on eBay. There is a wide variety of buyers and prices.

Emergence of 'infomediaries'

While many companies are under pressure from the Internet, it's clear that a new type of intermediary is emerging, sometimes called 'infomediary' in the jargon of the Internet. An infomediary is a company that brings information together from many different sources and presents it to Web users in a useful way.

For example, eBay is a company that holds no stock and ships nothing, but it provides buyers and sellers with the information they

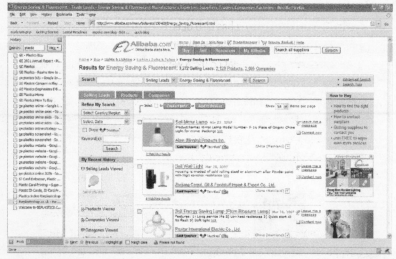

Alibaba.com is a website which allows commercial buyers to source products from thousands of manufacturers, mainly in China. Many manufacturers are prepared to fulfil relatively small orders.

need to sell and ship goods to one another, with eBay receiving a commission for each purchase. Similarly, Amazon.com does not keep all the items on its database in stock; many of them are obtained only when a customer requests them, and they may even be 'drop-shipped' directly from the publisher's warehouse to the end-customer. Many small companies provide a similar service; they run a website to market, sell and provide customer service for products, but the actual shipment of the goods is handled by another company.

More and more specialised intermediaries are also coming on the scene. One example is the phenomenon of 'group coupons' provided by Citydeals in Europe and Groupon in the United States. The group coupon is a special offer that is available once a group of people of a certain size agree to participate. An example might be the running of a cookery class, if a sufficient number of participants can be found. The same technique has also been used to market restaurants and 'experience' goods such as beauty treatments.

Another example is just-eat.co.uk, a website in the UK and Ireland that lets you order food for delivery online from a wide variety of restaurants in your area. Another more upmarket version of the same idea is Toptable in the UK and OpenTable in the US. These services allow prospective customers to find out what restaurant tables are available on a particular night.

Better service and mass customisation

Manufacturers and distributors are no longer able to rely on having an acceptable product at a reasonable price to sustain their sales. Cheaper substitutes are coming in from the Far East and are being distributed through discounters on the high street and online through eBay and Alibaba.com.

As a result, they are looking at new ways to make sure they retain their market leadership. The key strategies include:

- **increased emphasis on service.** Customers are now willing to pay a bit more for a product if it's supplied with all the services they need to set it up and keep it in operation. As well as attracting extra revenue, this approach builds a stronger connection with the product's users and creates 'lock-in', making it more difficult for the customer to simply shift to another supplier.
- **customised products.** New manufacturing techniques make it easier to produce goods to the exact specification of a customer, rather than providing them with something off the shelf. Modern factories allow this tailoring to be done at little extra expense.

When you place an order for an Apple computer from their website, it is built to your specifications and shipped directly. This allows Apple to minimise inventory and distribution costs and maximise the margin.

The demand for something different is difficult for mass producers to cater for at the outset. However, it can offer opportunities to smaller players who are often better versed at providing high-quality service to customers.

Access to a global marketplace

Small businesses have always been constrained by geography – that is, they generally can only sell to customers who are located near to them. The only way to extend into new territories was to open offices there or find a local distributor.

Today, a website is a shopfront that is open to the world. If you offer something distinct and different that is of interest to people from many different countries, then you are likely to get access to markets abroad.

But while borders are certainly coming down, there are many practical issues that you have to deal with when you do business in another country. There are still customs and tax issues to consider. Product safety and environmental standards may vary in different countries, and these issues need to be dealt with where they arise. Another consideration is how you can collect payments from abroad, and how to ship the goods.

Increased competition

The business world is getting increasingly competitive. Customers have access to more information about products and prices than ever before, and they have direct access to manufacturers and international distributors. The extension of international free trade arrangements, particularly the accession of Eastern European countries to the European Union, and the opening up of markets to Far Eastern countries, has further increased the pressure.

The importance of brand

With the advent of the Internet, brands have become ever more important. Customers prefer to buy products or services that come with a brand because:

■ they are overwhelmed with information and choice,
and like to use names they trust. Shoppers don't have
the time to spend ordering, waiting for, and then
testing out unrecognised brands. (In contrast, there
are many small companies with unfamiliar names that
are successfully selling software online – the Internet
makes it easy for purchasers to download and test
trial versions of software without having to commit to
a purchase.)

■ with so many channels available to consumers now,
they want to buy quality products they can rely on.
They believe that they can trust a recognised brand,
whether it's available through retail, a manufacturer's
website, a foreign retailer's website or eBay.

Information is part of the product

The information attached to a product or service is increasingly
important. For example, in the food industry, the documentation
and labelling regarding food origin and food safety measures are
critical to bringing the food successfully to market. The safety
certification and other information that comes with a piece of
machinery are as important to the end-customer as the product
itself.

Small businesses and the Internet

All these changes have had a big impact on some categories of
small business. As time goes on, this will further increase, and
owners of small businesses ignore what is happening at their peril.
The effects will be manifold:

- customers of small businesses will realise that they can get similar goods direct from a large international distributor rather than through a local agent. Unless the small company adds something that the big company cannot provide, the small business will inevitably lose out to its larger competitors on price and availability of supplies.

- service companies will have to compete in a marketplace where there is a greater depth of information available. Customers will be able to find out what other users of the service think, through discussion boards and consumer ratings sites. Information on company websites may colour their thinking.

Yelp is a website containing information and reviews about local businesses in the US, UK and Ireland.

MAKING AN IMPACT ONLINE

As larger companies get better at providing high-quality services and customising the products they sell, small businesses will lose their traditional edge. For example, in the personal computer business, locally built computers used to account for a significant part of the market. However, Dell, through its mass customisation

In the future, customers will increasingly look for positive reviews or endorsements before engaging a contractor.

strategy and its low-cost, high-volume production systems, now competes head-on with these small players, and the latter are finding it increasingly difficult to compete.

Previously, small players in this industry could dance around the big players, by keeping their overheads tighter, having a range of goods tailored to their clientele, and by providing knowledgeable and

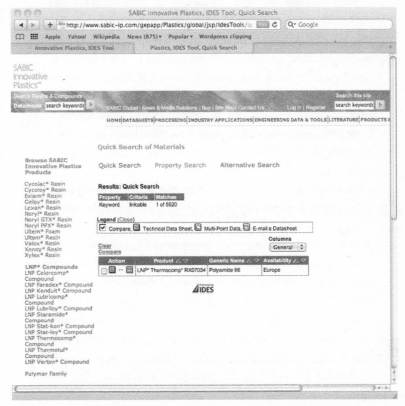

The Sabic Plastics (formerly GE Plastics) website allows their customers to find and order the exact products they need and access all the relevant information. They can also track the current orders.

friendly customer service. But online companies such as Amazon.com provide much stiffer competition. Their sites incorporate extensive information and reviews about their products, and although buying on the Internet does not have the immediacy of buying in a local shop, the range of goods offered is often unbeatable, and the cost of operations is lower than even the most economic high street operation.

These changes are also happening in business-to-business marketplaces. Large companies are modifying their systems so that they can deal with their customers in a more efficient and tailored manner, resulting in higher customer satisfaction and lower costs. Companies like Sabic Innovative (formerly GE Plastics) are now recording billions of dollars of sales per year through their website. They also offer services such as 'vendor inventory management'. Customers using this service have their stock levels of products automatically monitored by Sabic Innovative, to ensure that they never run out.

More and more business sectors will be affected in the coming years, as technology improves and more people gain access to the Internet.

An Internet strategy for *your* small business

As a businessperson, you probably already know about many of these changes. It's important to understand them and then decide how to deal with them. Although this is a dangerous time for a small business, it's also an opportunity for improvement and growth. To succeed, you will have to be flexible, and be prepared to change your strategy. The strategy you choose will depend on your situation, but here are a few key ideas for getting your business to adapt.

Establish your brand

Establish a brand that your customers can easily recognise, both on the Internet and off. Having a domain name, a website (even a simple one) and a logo will give your company greater credibility in the eyes of your existing customers as well as new ones. Likewise, it will make your business appear more credible to overseas suppliers or customers. A website will help them better understand your needs or the services you offer. It also provides a basis for expanding into selling or providing other services online, if that is appropriate for your business.

Chapter 2 outlines the basics of how to get a domain name and set up an e-mail account and a website. This is the foundation of your brand in the online world.

Listen and talk to your customers

Your existing and prospective customers are experts in what they need. Customers like to be listened to. They like to have their needs and ideas taken into account, so listen to what they say and try to meet their requirements.

The Internet makes customers powerful, and if they don't get the information or products they want from you, they will go to the Internet and find them there. Domestic *and* international competitors could then exploit an unanswered need to enter your market.

If your customers have questions about your product or your business, you have to be able to answer these promptly and accurately. If you can, use e-mail and the Web to communicate with them, for efficiency and speed.

If you can build a rapport with customers in this way, you reduce the likelihood that they will move away from you unexpectedly. Previously, you would have needed to have a significant sales force on the road to maintain a relationship with so many people. Now it's different: with e-mail and blogs, you can have a conversation with your customers much more easily and cost-effectively. As before, relationships are all-important.

Chapter 3 provides an approach to marketing on the Internet. Marketing is not just about telling customers and prospective customers what you offer; it's also about listening to the marketplace and finding out what those customers actually want from you.

Find your competitive advantage

Go through your customer lists and your recent invoices, and ask yourself, what is it that my company can do that no one else can do for my customers? What keeps them coming back? Why don't they just do business with one of the larger competitors?

You may discover that you have some unique advantage which you don't fully appreciate and exploit. For example, you may have key members of staff who are well known for their expertise and attention to customers. Maybe you can provide a specific product that isn't available anywhere else? Perhaps you are the only company providing your type of service within driving distance?

Whatever advantage your company has, think about how you can develop it, and exploit it. You might have to step up training to keep the edge your personnel currently hold. If you have a strong presence in a particular part of the country, consider providing extra products or services to the customers in this area.

The Internet should be an important part of finding and exploiting your niche. You may be able to use it to introduce your distinctive offering to a whole new market, or to source and introduce new products to your existing customers.

Get better information for your businesses

Business nowadays is increasingly about information. Make sure you are getting the information you need and that you are managing it efficiently. It will make you more sensitive to the changes that are happening in the marketplace. The key areas of information a small business may need are as follows:

■ **information about the products you supply and about your suppliers.** Having detailed information on hand will allow you to respond more rapidly to your customers' questions and requests for new products. Depending on your type of business, you may have to explain your standard operating procedures or your production processes.

■ **information about your customers.** It's critical to keep track of the names and contact details of your customers and the products they buy. This allows you to keep in regular contact with them and to serve their needs better.

■ **information about the market.** Marketplaces are constantly changing, with new competitors, new products and changes in customers' buying habits.

■ **financial, legal and safety information.** The government requires you to keep a host of records about your business.

It isn't enough to just have this information; it's essential to organise it and distribute it to the people who need it. Everyone involved has to be able to understand the information and use it to make appropriate decisions. Equally, confidential information has to be properly guarded.

Get the best deals and be more efficient
As your customers demand better service at a better price, consider whether your existing suppliers are providing the best price and

service to you. Like your customers, you can search on the Internet to make sure you are getting a good deal. You can use the same tools your customers are using to make contact with potential new suppliers.

The Internet can provide a means for you to completely reinvent your business. Amazon.com and Ryanair use the Internet to service customers' needs in a radically new way, and as a result they have succeeded in opening up completely new markets.

Chapter 4 explains how to go about implementing technology solutions in your business. Chapter 5 explains how to review your business to understand how it can use the Internet to become more streamlined and efficient.

Take advantage of your business's compact size

A focused strategy is important to give your business a long-term sustainable advantage in the Internet age. It will enable you to take advantage of your small size to compete in ways that your larger counterparts cannot. For example, you can keep in close contact with your customer, and it's easier for you to correct problems when they go wrong.

2

THE BASICS: SORT OUT A DOMAIN NAME, AN E-MAIL ACCOUNT, A WEBSITE, AND GET SELLING

Every business, even one operating on a shoestring, should have some basic tools to get going on the Internet. Simple things, like a memorable domain name and individual e-mail addresses, will give your customers and suppliers a professional impression of your business. They needn't be expensive, but it's important to get them right.

Broadband

The first step is to sort out your Internet access. If your don't have Internet access at all in your business, or if you are making do with an old-fashioned dialup connection (where your phone is out of action while you plug into the phone line), you should consider getting broadband connection. There are a number of business benefits:

- a broadband connection will probably cost the same as or less than a dial-up connection if you use it more than two or three times per day
- you will save time by being able to access Web pages more quickly and to download and send e-mails much more rapidly
- you will be able to easily share the connection between all the users in your office

Choosing a broadband provider and service

The easiest option is to buy a broadband package from your current phone company. The charge will go on your regular bill and the phone company should take care of most of the technical details of setting everything up. It is a competitive marketplace, however, and you do have a choice about where you get your broadband. You may have a special reason for choosing another provider. If you decide to get another company to provide the service, it may involve more paperwork and it may take that bit longer to set up.

The main difference between the different services available is the speed, which is expressed in megabits per second (Mbps for short). This represents the maximum amount of data that can be downloaded through the Internet connection. This number is not a hard-and-fast guide to how good a service you can get. For a start, it's a theoretical number; you will generally not get the full nominal capacity of your line, because some of it will be used for signalling, error-checking and other technical purposes.

The speed available to you depends on two factors: the quality of the connection into your premises, and the package you choose. You may be on a 20 Mbps package, but if the phone line into your office is only capable of carrying 7 Mbps, then 7 Mbps is the maximum you will ever receive. There are many reasons why one line may be better than another, but the most important factor is how far you are from the phone exchange.

A 5 Mbps service (or possibly even lower) is perfectly adequate to start off with for small businesses with a few users. You will need a higher bandwidth service if:

- **you download a lot of large files (video, images, etc.)**
- **your business depends on sending large files to clients**
- **you have more than two or three employees accessing the Internet at once**

Some services also have bandwidth restrictions, or 'caps'. If you download more than a certain amount, you risk an extra charge. For most customers, however, this will not be an issue.

Many Internet service providers (ISPs) provide a domain name, e-mail hosting (sometimes called POP3/SMTP; see p. 36) and Web hosting (sometimes called Web space), of which more later, as part of their service, and this may be a consideration when you are choosing your provider. However, these services can also be purchased separately, at quite a low price, and so this should not be your first priority.

Some ISPs offer a firewall service. This is a security service, designed to protect your network against unauthorised attempts to connect to your company's network. In practice, these services are often poor value for small companies. Most ADSL (asymmetric digital subscriber line) modems – which connect your computer to the Internet – contain basic firewall functionality which may be adequate for your needs. No firewall service will protect you against all the risks of being on the Internet, however, so do take care.

Taking security seriously

Every business needs to take computer security seriously. For most companies, the most important precaution is to have a good anti-virus scanner installed on every Microsoft Windows-based computer and make sure its database of viruses (Virus Definition File) is updated every day. However, virus scanners are never a complete solution. For one thing, they only check for viruses that have already been identified by the anti-virus vendor and will not detect ones that have only just been released. They also do not provide protection against non-virus threats, such as hackers.

The best advice to avoid security problems is for you and your staff to be cautious and sensible. You should only open or download files which you are reasonably sure you can rely on. If you receive attachments from anonymous sources, or from websites which you don't know to be reputable, don't open them: you're running a large (and potentially very expensive) risk.

Have your computers set up to receive updates from Microsoft or Apple. New security problems (called 'security holes') are constantly emerging, and software companies provide fixes (also called 'hotfixes' or 'patches') to deal with the problem. On Microsoft Windows systems, for example, the Automatic Updates control panel allows you to check whether your computer is set correctly to automatically download security fixes from Microsoft.

Use secure passwords

Also take some time to set your passwords carefully: if they can be easily guessed, your security can be easily compromised. For maximum security, passwords should have at least six characters and contain a combination of letters and numbers. It is also wise to change them regularly.

Train your staff

Not everybody in your company is going to be as conscientious as the owner and manager about the problems of computer security. Everyone needs to know how important it is to take these basic precautions. Take the time to explain to everybody who works with you that the above security precautions are critical for your firm.

When do you need more security?

The tips above should cater for most eventualities. However, you will need extra security expertise if computers connected to the Internet are used for any of the following:

- storing sensitive personal data (this could include financial data, medical data, or legal briefs)
- storing critical trade secrets that need to be protected
- controlling critical equipment (for example, machinery in a factory, or electrical systems)

Contention

Contention is to do with the number of users who are sharing (contending for) the same bandwidth. A broadband connection is 'contended' if you have to share the bandwidth with other broadband customers in your area.

For most small businesses, contention is unlikely to be an issue because not everyone is using the bandwidth at the same time.

However, if the bandwidth is being shared between too many people, or if you need to continuously download very large files at high speed, it could easily become a concern.

Cable and wireless broadband services

Until relatively recently the only option for most small businesses was to buy broadband services from a phone company and the service was delivered through the telephone wire. Now, there are a number of options:

- **Wireless.** Wireless broadband companies can provide a service through a discreet antenna located in your premises. This may be located indoors or outdoors, depending on your location. The benefit of wireless service is typically price and availability. The service may be cheaper than other providers (although watch out for installation fees which may increase the overall price) and it may be available in areas where there are no other broadband options. The downside is sometimes reliability. As wireless networks get busier and more congested, they may slow down or even suffer from breaks in service.
- **Cable.** Many cable television companies now provide broadband services. As well as offering good prices, cable TV

companies can use their modern infrastructure to provide far higher connection speeds than can be delivered either wirelessly or through the telephone line. However, contention is more likely to be a problem on this type of connection than with a phone service. Also, bear in mind that cable companies are often relatively new and less business-focused than their telephone company competitors, and as a result may be less focused on providing high quality customer service.

■ **Mobile.** The major mobile operators also offer broadband using their 3G networks. This is similar to wireless broadband, with the added advantage that you can use the service on a laptop when you are out and about, not just when you are in the office or at home. If you work a lot on the road using a laptop computer, this is certainly invaluable. You can also access the 3G network to deal with emails and browse the web quite well from the new generations of Apple and Android mobile phones. Many phones can also be 'tethered' to a laptop to allow Internet access through the phone's 3G connection.

The downside is that mobile connections are not always dependable and are not particularly fast (although it very much depends on where you are located at the time).

If you depend heavily on the Internet, need to send a lot of emails, use the web a lot or especially if you need to download large files, a 3G connection will probably not be sufficient in itself and you will also need a more permanent connection in your office.

Hardware

You will need a device to act as an interface between your phone line and your computer network. This device is called a broadband modem, or a broadband router, because its main function is to 'route' small packets of information in the correct direction. You can buy your own broadband router, but in general it's simplest to use one supplied by the ISP. That way, if there are any problems with your service, your ISP will be willing to diagnose problems with the hardware. This can save a lot of time and hassle.

Support

If you're not an expert on setting up broadband and networks, you will be depending on your ISP's support line at some point to get your connection up and running and to deal with any problems that arise. Different ISPs have very different levels of service, and this should be an important criterion when making your decision. Some ISPs have a premium number for technical support, which means that you have to pay for every minute you are on the phone line to them. You can be held in a queue on the phone for some time before you can get access to someone who can help you with your problem, which can be nerve-wracking if you are in a hurry. The most important thing, though, is the quality of the technical support staff – and it's hard to find out how good they actually are at their jobs until you run into difficulty.

If support is important to you, ask around and find out which companies other businesses recommend, and the companies who get good reviews for their technical support.

Setting it up

Once you have ordered your broadband, it will take at least a few days to set up on your line and deliver a broadband modem to your premises. If you already have an office network, getting it put on the Internet should not be too complex if you follow the ISP's instructions. If you don't have an office network, then the first step is to get one computer on the Internet. When you're comfortable with that, decide whether it would be useful for you to buy any extra hardware or cabling to get all the computers in your office online. Once your computers are all connected to each other, they will all be able to get access to the Internet.

If you are new to computer networking, you will probably want to get someone more skilled to help you. Some ISPs provide installation services, and this may be the fastest way to get up and running. Alternatively, you may need the help of an IT contractor, who will also be willing to do other set-up work, such as installing a network, or setting up antivirus software.

For information and reviews of ISPs in the UK, visit: www. ispreview.co.uk/

Your domain name

Once you have Internet access, it's time to think about how you might present your company on the Internet. The first thing to consider is your domain name. Next, you need to set up your Internet e-mail and your website to work with that domain name.

What's a domain name?

The domain name system (DNS) makes it easier for people to use the Internet without having to remember or write down complex strings of numbers.

Every computer on the Internet has a unique address, called an IP (Internet protocol) address. You will occasionally come across these numbers when configuring your computer and they appear in forms such as 192.168.0.1 or 159.134.237.6. They are like a telephone number for computers, and are used to direct information to and from the correct destination when you access a website or send an e-mail.

A domain name is designed to be easier to remember than an IP address. The DNS takes a domain name (which people understand) and translates it into IP numbers (which computers understand). When you type in a domain name (for example, www.eire.com or www.google.co.uk) your computer looks up that name in the DNS, which translates it into an IP number (such as 80.169.141.78 or 66.102.9.104). Your computer then accesses that IP number to fetch the Web page you require. Domain names are also used to deliver e-mail to the right address, and for countless other Internet applications.

The domain name system is a little like a telephone directory, translating between names and numbers. Getting yourself listed is called 'registering a domain name'. The whole system is overseen by an organisation called ICANN (Internet Corporation for Assigned Names and Numbers).

Rather than being a single big directory for all of the names, however, the system is divided up into 'top level domains' (TLDs), such as **.com, .org, .ie, .uk** and so on. ICANN delegates the operation of each top level domain to a registry. The registry for **.com** is a US company, Verisign. For **.uk**, the registry is Nominet (although **.ac.uk** addresses are administered by ja.net, the education and research networking organisation, and **.gov.uk** domains managed by the Cabinet Office). These registries take care of applications for domains. So, for example, if you want to register the domain name **joesdiner.co.uk**, the relevant agency to deal with the registration will be Nominet, to which the **.uk** domain is delegated.

The benefits of having a domain name
For a fairly small fee, you can get an ISP to register a domain name
for you and have it connected to your website and e-mail. This has
the following advantages.

- Your e-mail addresses and Web addresses look distinctive and
  professional.
- Rather than having a generic e-mail address (such as
  fredcooke@bt.com or maryk@yahoo.co.uk) or a generic Web
  hosting address (like www.easynet.co.uk/fredsplumbers) you
  and your employees' addresses have a clear connection with
  your business. For example, if you get the domain name
  fredsplumbers.co.uk, you can then set up whatever e-mail
  addresses you wish (such as **fred@fredsplumbers.co.uk**, or
  mary@fredsplumbers.co.uk).
- You can change your e-mail and Web hosting company
  quite easily and bring your domain name with you (an
  e-mail address which contains the domain name of your ISP,
  or an Internet e-mail provider like Hotmail, Yahoo! or Gmail is
  tied to the company who issued it to you, and you cannot
  move it).
- It's more memorable then an e-mail address containing the
  name of an ISP.

Checking and registering domain names
You can quickly check whether a domain name is
available using the following websites. Remember to

check only the domain name (for example, domain.co. uk, or domain.com, *not* www.domain.co.uk or www. domain.com).

Nominet is responsible for domain names ending in .co. uk, .org.uk, .ltd.co.uk and .plc.co.uk: www.nominet.org.uk/

IE Domain Registry Ltd manages domain names ending in .ie (for Ireland): www.domainregistry.ie/

Internic is operated by ICANN, the body responsible for domain names internationally. This site provides information about the availability of .com, .org and .net domain names: www.internic.net/whois.html

Although the above organisations are responsible for overall management, you should not approach them in relation to registering a domain name. It is better to deal with a hosting provider (such as blacknight.com) who will deal in turn with these bodies on your behalf. More details about choosing a hosting company are provided in the next section.

Choosing a good domain name

Your domain name must not have been taken by someone else already. While domain names are frequently traded, it will probably be difficult for you to get the domain name you want if it is already taken. However, if a particular domain that you are interested in is 'parked' you could try to buy it. Take care that the person you are buying it from has the right to sell it, and that he or she actually hands it over at the conclusion of the deal.

1. Use a domain name that is recognisable to your customers

The first guideline for choosing a domain name is obvious. Get a domain name that is similar to your current brand or trademark and that will be easily recognised by your existing customers. How is your company known to your customers at the moment? That should be the key to choosing the name. Of course, you are probably going to have to compromise: **smiths.co.uk** may not be available, but **smithshardware.co.uk** or **smithskeycutting. co.uk** might be.

2. Use generic names with caution

If you trade as Tavistock Plumbing Supplies, concentrate on getting a domain name such as **tavistockplumbing.co.uk** or **tavistockplumbing.com**, rather than something like **plumbingsupplies.co.uk** which your customers will have difficulty in associating with your business.

On the other hand, if you are starting a business from scratch that will be focused on the Internet, a generic name like **plumbingsupplies. co.uk** might be a good idea. Beware though; these generic names are not easy to protect if there is a dispute. So if a competitor were to open up under the name **plumbingandgeneralsupplies.co.uk**, or **plumbingsuppliesdover.co.uk**, it would be very difficult to do anything about it, because the name is so general and non-specific to your business.

If you have the opportunity to acquire generic domain names, you could buy them and just put up a simple Web page, with a link on the site to your own main website. That way you get any benefit that arises from potential customers simply typing the generic term into their browser window, without necessarily having to make the investment in marketing it.

3. Make it short, snappy and memorable

Technically speaking, domain names can contain more than 60 characters, but shorter ones are easier to remember and are less likely to be misspelt.

Your company may be known by a shortened name or a nickname to your customers – if so, consider using that as your domain name or as part of it. For example, **bbc.co.uk** is much easier to remember, and to type correctly, than **thebritishbroadcastingcorporation.co.uk**.

4. Avoid hyphens, prefixes, suffixes and numerals if you can

Although hyphens and numerals are permitted in domain names, they may not be easy for your customers to remember or to type. Other symbols are generally not permitted in domain names (although this is changing).

Likewise, numerals are allowed in domain names, and sometimes they are used to replace words. For example, the domain name 'furniture4u.com' is a shortened version of 'furniture for you'. However, these domain names may be hard to remember for non-net-savvy customers.

Use plurals and prefixes like 'the' and 'my' only if you have no choice. Customers are more likely to remember the name without them.

Internationalised Domain Names (IDNs)

Until recently, there was no way to have any character other than the letters A to Z, numerals 1 to 9 and a hyphen in a domain name. But with the increasing use of the Internet in Asia and other countries where the Roman alphabet is not widely used, there is a need to be able to use the characters of all the languages in a domain name and IDNs are just becoming available.

Internationalised domain names may be important for your company if you do a lot of business with other countries and in a language where non-roman characters are used.

The IDN project is arranging the technical modifications that are necessary to make this happen. Changes need to be made at all levels: to the domain name registries, the registrars, the Web browsers and the operating systems of the users' computers. The policy on making them available, therefore, depends on the individual domain registrar.

5. Use a conventional top-level domain if you can

Domain names are arranged into various levels (**.com, .org, .co.uk**, etc.). Use a top-level domain (TLD) that your customers are likely to be used to. Typically, this will mean **.com**, or **.co.uk** or **.ie**. That said, it can be very difficult to get short, snappy **.com** domain names. There is nothing wrong with other TLDs such as **.biz, .info** and so on, although customers are less likely to recognise and remember them.

6. Brainstorm

Don't fret if the name you really want isn't available. Talk to employees, friends and others to get their views and see what alternatives come to mind.

7. Have more than one domain name (but focus on one)

It is possible to get yourself more than one domain name. In fact, you can get several and keep them in reserve (although you will need to pay yearly fees to keep them in operation and to maintain control of them).

Your primary interest may be to get a domain with the appropriate ending for your country such as **.ie, .co.uk** and so on, but it is worth trying to get the **.com, .net, .org** or other domain name as well if you can, so that it's easier for customers to find you. However, concentrate your efforts on marketing just one of these, unless your business is big or diverse enough to really need two domain names.

Registering and hosting your domain name

You don't register your domain name directly with the company that runs the top-level domain (called the 'registry'), but rather through an ISP or hosting company which will deal with the registry on your behalf. The ISP or hosting company will also provide e-mail and Web services for that domain.

What is a 'host'?

A 'host' is a technical term for a computer that is permanently connected to the Internet and which provides (or 'hosts') services which other computers on the Internet access. For example, every website resides on an Internet-connected computer somewhere. Similarly, when you send an e-mail, there has to be a computer waiting ready to receive it and store it until the recipient is ready to read it. A host is often referred to as a 'server' too.

Any computer connected to the Internet can act as a host, at least in theory. However, it's a lot more practical to get a specialised company to provide this service. These companies can offer the following benefits:

- **high level of Internet connectivity.** Even a small hosting company will have better Internet connectivity than you do at your office. Your office may have a 30 or 50 Mbps connection at best. The hosting company will have a 100 Mbps, Gigabit or bigger connection available to its customers.
- **redundancy.** In computing, redundancy means having back-up systems available. For example, a hosting company will have more than one connection to the Internet. Similarly it will have a back-up power system, using a UPS (uninterruptible power supply, which is basically a giant battery that keeps systems running during a power cut), diesel generators and multiple connections to the power company.
- **staffing.** Hosting companies have technical staff on hand to design and maintain their networks, and to deal with emergencies.
- **flexibility.** If your site suddenly becomes massively popular, the hosting company is likely to have the capacity to deal with it.
- **safe location.** A hosting company is usually located in a secure hosting centre which has security systems and fire containment systems to minimise the chance of any incidents.
- **price.** Since the hosting business is competitive and because it operates on a large scale, hosting deals are relatively inexpensive, and start at less than £20 a month.

Choosing a hosting company

If possible, select a single hosting service to provide all your domain hosting, Web hosting and e-mail hosting needs, and then stick with them. It is technically feasible to spread the job amongst a number of different companies, but it will make it difficult or confusing for you when it comes to making changes. Rather than having to deal with one company, you will have to deal with a number of them, and it can be easy to forget to do something important (such as pay a bill for a particular domain name) which can easily result in your e-mail account being frozen and also make the administration much more difficult.

If your domain name expires without notice (for example, if you fail to get a bill because you have moved office or changed e-mail address), it could cause serious disruption for your business. Similarly, if your hosting company suddenly stops trading, it may be difficult to get in touch with someone who can help deal with any problems you have. If the company doesn't have good customer service, it may be difficult to upgrade your account or make other changes.

On the technical side, if the company you choose gets a sudden spurt of growth, the quality of the service may decrease while it rushes to upgrade its systems.

In practice, you have to add up the pros and cons. Big hosting companies tend to be the most reliable and best able to deal with major growth. Smaller companies tend to have a more personalised customer service and are more likely to go out of their way to help you.

What services will the hosting company provide?

A good hosting company will provide the following:

■ **domain names.** The hosting company will apply to the domain name registry on your behalf and deal with

the bureaucracy of getting your domain name. It will
then host your domain, which means that its computers
will respond every time someone types in the domain
name of your website, or sends an e-mail to your domain
e-mail address. The domain name will then be converted
into an IP address of the server computer which has
your website stored on it or which will handle your
incoming e-mail.

■ **an e-mail service.** When someone sends an e-mail to
your domain, it is dealt with by your hosting company's
e-mail server. The e-mail server takes delivery of the e-mail
and then stores it in a mailbox for you until you download it
and deal with it. It may also forward your outgoing e-mail to
its final destination. Alternatively, your ISP may provide this
service.

You should be able to set up 10 or 20 e-mail addresses on your
hosting account for yourself and your employees. Each of these
should have individual e-mail mailboxes.

The service of receiving and forwarding e-mail is referred to as
SMTP (simple mail transfer protocol). The storage of e-mail in
mailboxes is sometimes called POP3 (post office protocol). There is
an advanced version of this service called IMAP (interactive mail
access protocol), which has the advantage of allowing read mail to
be stored on the server rather than on your computer.

There are some added e-mail features that some hosts may
provide, and which may be relevant for you:

■ **Web-based e-mail.** A Web-based e-mail system allows
employees to access each other's e-mails when they are
away from their computers. They simply go to a special

Web address, enter their username and password and
see any new e-mail on-screen.

■ **spam-checking.** A good mail hosting service will
include a feature for checking for spam (unsolicited junk
e-mails), making it easy for you to filter it out in your mail
program. However no spam program is perfect and there is
always the possibility that some spam will get through or —
worse still — that some legitimate messages will be marked as
spam. Many systems now have a control panel, however, that
allows you to look through the messages identified as spam
and release any that are from customers or clients that you
recognise.

Web hosting

All hosting companies will provide you with basic Web space for
your domain. However, there are a few technical things you need to
know in order to understand the differences between the various
packages on offer:

■ **Web space.** This is the amount of space on the disks of the
hosting company's computer allocated for your use. Disk space
is cheap these days, so a space of 100 megabytes or more is
not unusual. A typical basic website will generally only need a
few megabytes.

■ **bandwidth allowance.** All hosting companies impose
some limit on the amount of traffic your website can
receive in a month. Unless you are offering very large
files for download, or your site suddenly becomes very
popular, you are unlikely to need a very high bandwidth
allowance at the outset. You can always upgrade later if
necessary.

- **scripting (also known as 'server side scripting').** If your site has more complex features, such as e-mail forms or some sort of search system, you will need to be able to put scripts on your site. Not all hosting plans allow this. There are a number of different scripting languages in common use (for example, PHP, Perl, ASP and JSP) and although they all do more or less the same job, they aren't compatible with each other so you need to be sure that the hosting company offers the one you require. If you plan to use Microsoft Frontpage, it's a good idea to ask about Microsoft Frontpage Support. Your Web developer will probably be responsible for making the decision about what scripting language to use. Don't bother with this extra feature if you aren't fairly sure you'll actually need it.

- **databases.** More complex sites will require a database such as MySQL, PostgreSQL or Microsoft SQL Server to store detailed, structured information and allow it to be retrieved easily. Your Web developer will be able to tell you whether this is needed. If you are uncertain, you will be able to upgrade later if necessary.

- **dedicated hosting/ co-located hosting.** The standard hosting service offered to small businesses is for shared hosting, which means your website and e-mail is kept on a server that is also used by other customers of the hosting company. This is to keep costs down, and as each customer uses only a small fraction of the available capacity, the arrangement usually works very well. However, if you need special software, or require a lot of disk space or bandwidth, you may be better off getting a server of your own. This server is then 'dedicated' for your use, but is 'co-located' at the premises of the hosting company, so that it can utilise the redundant broadband and power connections available there.

- **Windows or Unix hosting.** Most hosting companies offer a choice of having your site hosted on a Windows or a Unix system. Windows is the operating system that is familiar to almost all computer users. Unix is the operating system that is generally used for large-scale websites. There are a number of 'varieties' of Unix, the best known being Linux. Unless it's absolutely vital that you use a scripting language that is only available on Windows, it doesn't really matter which one you choose, and you should probably go for whichever is more economic.
- **e-commerce hosting.** Most companies offer a deal which includes an SSL (secure sockets layer) server certificate and some type of online shopping software with their hosting package. (An SSL server will encrypt data in order to protect it during transmission.) You should only take this service if your Web developer says you need it. It is possible to establish a simple e-commerce site without having a special hosting set-up.

There are a number of other aspects of a hosting company or package that you should take into account before you sign up.

Customer service features

Having access to a simple way of making changes to your set-up, for example adding or deleting an e-mail address, or resetting an e-mail password, will make your life a lot easier. Some companies require you to telephone the help desk to make these changes, but it is far better if you can make them yourself, using a control panel.

Good telephone support

If you are setting up a domain for the first time, you may need some help with setting up your domain, setting up e-mail addresses and configuring the mail program on your computer to work with the service. Even if you are technically inclined, you will always run into hiccups. Try to find out whether the company provides good customer support. Depending on your technical ability, you may want to pay extra if you know you are going to get good technical service.

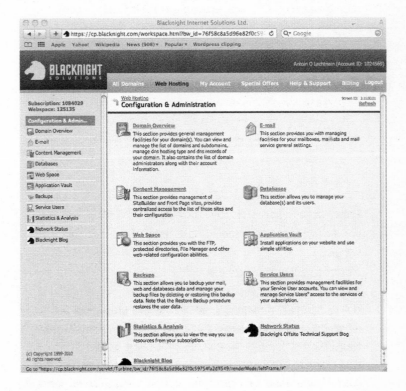

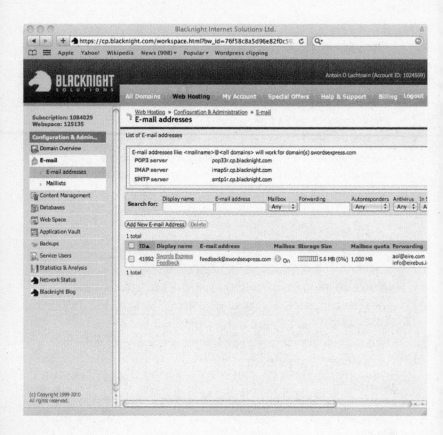

Reputation and longevity

You want to be confident that your hosting company is going to stay in business. If there is a problem, it may take some time to regain control of your domain name and move it to a new hosting company.

Location

If possible, you should host with a company in the same part of the world as you. While you can get excellent deals, from American providers in particular, you may run into difficulties with payments, support hours and familiarity with the procedures for registering **.uk** and **.ie** domain names.

Competitive pricing

There is a lot of competition in the marketplace, so you should be able to get the hosting service you want at a very good price. Hosting will probably cost less than your broadband Internet access package.

Free hosting services

If you are really stuck for cash, you can get free e-mail and Web hosting from a number of sources, possibly including your own ISP. But do think about whether this free deal is really good value. The following are the issues you are likely to encounter.

- **You may not be able to use your own domain name. If you are, you will still have to pay for maintenance of the domain name.**
- **There will be little or no technical support or customer service.**
- **The service is more likely to be terminated without notice. Obviously this would be disastrous if you depend on your website for your business.**

Google and hosting

Google can provide some of your hosting needs through 'Google Apps'. This service is provided for free for organisations with up to 10 users (i.e. 10 people with e-mail addresses).

As with other free offerings, the main disadvantage is that there is very little customer support offered. In practice, this might be fine if you are comfortable dealing with all the technical details yourself, but you may prefer to pay for a service that offers ongoing support.

One shortcoming of Google Apps is that Google only sells a limited range of domain names. It offers .com, .org, .net, .info and .biz domain names, but does not offer country specific domains like .co.uk or .ie. However, if you have registered a domain with a hosting company, you can use this domain with Google Apps.

There is a lot more to Google Apps than just e-mail. Google Apps also provides online calendars, and Google Docs, Google's online replacement for traditional applications like Microsoft Word, Excel and PowerPoint. It also provides Google Sites, a basic facility for building your own website.

Develop your requirements checklist

Now that you understand the difference between the features and services of the different hosting options, you can set out finding the company that suits your needs.

The first step is to write down your requirements. These should be covered by the following questions:

1. **How many e-mail addresses do I need?** Reckon on having an e-mail address for everyone in your organisation who regularly sits at a desk. You may also want to provide e-mail addresses for contractors who frequently work with you. It's always best to have a few extra available to allow for expansion or unexpected needs.
2. **How much Web space do I need?** Unless you'll be wanting to put up large files, you will probably need around 10 or 20 megabytes.
3. **Do I need to use scripts?** Decide whether you are likely to use scripts, Frontpage or any other special technologies. What scripting languages do you need? (Ask your Web developer about this.)
4. **What level of customer service do I need?** Is it important to have a number you can call at evenings or weekends?
5. **What payment schedule and method suit me?** Do you want to pay monthly by credit card, or yearly in advance by cheque?

Create your shortlist

Once you have your requirements, create a shortlist of companies to consider in more depth. Here are the recommended steps.

Investigate hosting options with your ISP

The ISP you use for your broadband service may be able to provide hosting services, but this is not always the best option. The ISP may not be willing, or able, to provide control panels to allow self-service, or advanced services such as scripts or databases. In addition, the ISP's charges may be much higher than you could get from an independent hosting company. If the ISP's main focus is providing broadband services, they may not provide good-quality customer service for dealing with hosting issues.

Ask for recommendations

Ask your Web developer, if you have one, to recommend a hosting company. He or she may offer to take care of the hosting for you, but do look carefully at the ongoing price you will be charged: it might be cheaper to get the same service directly from the hosting company.

Your contacts are the best source of information about hosting companies, so ask other businesses which one they recommend. If possible, get opinions from other customers before you sign up. This is the best way to gauge whether the company is considered reliable and whether it provides good customer service and support.

Use an online list of hosts

There are a number of sites which provide information about hosting services. For the UK, for example, you could consult some of the following sites:

- **www.hostratings.co.uk**
- **www.webhostdir.co.uk**
- **http://huk.tophosts.com**

There are similar lists for many other countries, and you can find them quite quickly if you search on Google or Yahoo! for 'web hosting' in conjunction with the name of the country.

All of these sites contain basic information about the various companies offering hosting services. Be careful, though. Some of these sites are supported by advertising from the hosting companies, and so the information provided may be somewhat biased. Evaluate feedback from other customers carefully. Sometimes customers have unrealistic expectations about the level of service a hosting company can provide for a low price. It is important to be realistic about what you can expect from a very cut-price service.

Speak to hosting companies

Once you have your shortlist, you can evaluate the players in more detail. You could assess each company from its website alone, but it's usually better to ring and talk to someone so that you can get a better fix on what they're offering (and gain an insight into what their customer service standards are like to boot).

Use your requirements checklist to explain your situation to the salesperson at each company and ask him or her to recommend the hosting package which best suits your requirements. Find out what the complete price of the service will be, including any extras. Ask about the company itself – where it is located, how many people it employs, and what makes it distinctive from, or better than, the other providers in the market.

Check online feedback

Check what people are saying about the hosting companies you are interested in, by searching for their names on Google or Yahoo! You may get some indication as to whether customers are experiencing good service from each company. That said, you should not rely on Web searches alone; sometimes disgruntled customers make remarks about businesses that are unfair and personal. Equally, you should check that the comments you find are recent – the standard of management in a hosting company can change quite a lot over time.

Make a decision

Make a balanced decision based on your findings. Do take price into account, but don't make it the key differentiator. It's much more important to have a company you can rely upon and which provides all the features you need.

Staff issues and the Internet

If you are providing access to the Internet and e-mail for your staff, it's important to consider the issues involved and have a clear policy on how these resources should be used. Abuse of the Internet doesn't just waste time, it could cause embarrassment for your firm. There have been several incidents where relatively junior members of the staff of large companies sent e-mails containing off-colour jokes and very personal remarks which later became widely distributed and caused major embarrassment.

Typical behaviour that may upset staff and other contacts outside the company include:

- viewing adult material in the workplace
- sending inappropriate humorous material through the company e-mail system
- inappropriate or accidental sharing of gossip and scandal
- downloading copyright material from websites or file-sharing systems
- inappropriate use of social networking sites which effects the reputation of the company

■ **using the Internet for long periods for non-business-related matters**

Have a written policy containing clear guidelines. The policy should be shown to, and signed by, new employees before they start work.

Developing a computer use policy

Whether your business operates online or not, it's important that you draw up a comprehensive set of guidelines that make clear to your employees what you expect from them in terms of their computer and Internet use. Some companies expressly forbid staff from surfing during working hours, while others recognise that some Internet use is acceptable so long as it does not interfere with their jobs.

The UK government's Business Link advice site for small businesses has an extensive section on Internet access policies. Visit www.businesslink.gov.uk and select the 'IT and e-commerce' option on the left-hand menu.

This should be a helpful starting point as you begin to formulate your own thoughts and you can, of course, adapt it to your own business's specific needs. In broad strokes, however, remember to:

■ **make your final computer use policy a prominent part of your standard employee contract, so that all new staff know about it from the word go. Also explain the policy to any contractors or temporary employees who may use your business's e-mail services.**
■ **make it clear that Internet use may be monitored.**

- be realistic. It is generally accepted that employees are allowed to use Internet access from their desks for personal purposes.
- make sure you can follow through on your policy. If you receive complaints of abuse, be prepared to deal with them.
- report serious offences to the police, even if you have internal disciplinary procedures.

A website on a shoestring?

There is no reason why every business these days, even the smallest one, should not to have a basic website, even if it just runs to two or three pages. It gives your company an air of professionalism, and gives prospective customers a way to find out about your company without having to ring you up and engage directly with you.

At the most basic level, your site has to represent your business. It should look professional, bear your logo and articulate your basic marketing message. It should include all the basic information, such as your phone number, your location and the products or services you offer. Your needs may go even further than that. You may want to gather customer information, sell products online, or connect into the systems inside your business (such as ordering or financial programs).

Once you've decided what you want your site to do, you'll be in a position to choose a Web design company that can give you the best value for what you need.

How complex should your website be?

Your website is your shopfront on the Internet. At the most basic level, it should provide the following:

- a simple overview of your company and the products and services it offers
- contact details for your company, in sufficient detail for potential customers to be able to get in touch with you

There is nothing wrong with having a website that only provides this level of functionality. If your company is strongly oriented towards personal service and giving customers face-to-face attention, it may be all you ever need.

A more complex site might contain some of the following features:

- regularly updated information for your customers, partners and potential customers
- more detailed information about the products or services you are offering. For example, a car dealer could provide specifications on all the vehicles he has for sale at a given time; an estate agent might incorporate a complete listing of all available properties.
- the ability for customers to order products or book services online
- a discussion board or collaboration facility that allows customers or site visitors to interact with one another
- access to information databases of interest to your customers (for a manufacturer or distributor, this might include technical data sheets or other detailed product information; for a services company, it could be articles and news about the sector)

If your budget increases as time goes on, the features listed below would also be useful. Generally speaking, they are outside the capability of most small companies, but you could consider:

- connections into your company's or other companies' internal IT systems that allow customers to find out about the availability of services or stock within your company, and to check the progress of current orders
- configuration tools to allow customers to customise their orders for products and services, and have those orders automatically passed into your production systems

It's not necessary, or even a good idea, to develop a very complex website at the outset in order to get up and running online – many of the most successful websites come from quite humble beginnings. For example, although the founder of eBay had a technical background and was able to implement most of the website himself, the original eBay site did not have any payment facility built in (eBay only linked up with Paypal several years later). Similarly, the original Amazon.com site did not have any facility for checking whether a book was actually available or in stock, and credit-card orders had to be processed manually. Even today, the Tesco Home Delivery website is not fully tied into the stock control system of the stores.

High-level planning

Put together a written document detailing what you want from your website before you begin any actual development. This might seem like a waste of time – after all, you may feel that your requirements are quite clear. However, if you haven't been involved in designing a website before, you will be surprised at how tricky the process can be.

Even if you decide that your website requirements are simple, and you plan to develop your first site yourself, take the time to write down some answers to a few questions. Things which seem easy can turn out to be hard, and things that appear highly complex can turn out to be relatively simple. It can be very difficult to explain exactly what you want from the website to the other people who are working with you on the project.

At this stage of planning, it makes sense to describe your 'ideal' website. Although you may not be able to implement this at the outset, it helps to have a long-term vision for how the website might develop over time.

Website planning work plan

What is my website about?
Include a short description of your business as you wish to portray it on the Internet. It should cover the key points you want to make through the site to your target customers.

Who is my audience?
Is your site aimed at people who are knowledgeable about your products or service, or people who need to learn more? Is it aimed at existing customers, or at new ones? What kind of people are in the audience (young,

old, male, female)? If you can establish or validate this information through research with your colleagues or customers, so much the better, but to begin with, your best guess will do.

Professional Web developers sometimes invent 'user personas' to help guide the development. A user persona is simply an imaginary person, described as fully possible, who might be a typical user of the website. It helps to describe the user in terms of:

- job
- age
- family situation
- income
- what computer experience they have
- how often they use the Internet
- why they might have visited the site
- level of information sought

You might need to develop more than one persona for the site, but try to keep the number of personas to a minimum.

What do the audience want?

When your audience reaches your website, they almost certainly have some specific purpose in mind. What is it? Typical reasons why they might visit the site are:

- they want to buy something
- they want to find out a price

- they are looking for general information about the products or services that you sell
- they want to speak to someone knowledgeable
- they want to know more about your company

As with the user personas above, a technique called 'scenario development' can help Web developers flesh out their concept of their customers. This involves imagining a likely scenario in which your user persona might visit the site.

What are the objectives of my website?

How do you aim to serve the needs of the target audience? Your primary objective might be to get information about a particular topic to customers who are looking for it, so that they will become familiar with your company and your products or services. Or your primary priority might be to serve customers who are ready to make a purchase, by providing an online ordering facility. You may simply want to encourage visitors to make an enquiry, which will provide you with a sales lead to follow up.

What information will be on the site?

What type of information would your target audience like to see on the site? Typically, this will include a company description and contact details at the most basic level. Most sites will have descriptions of products and services. Some sites will have a wider range of product information. Think about the amount of information you plan to put on the site, and where it will come from.

What graphic elements will go into the site?
Do you have photographs, illustrations or even videos or DVDs that you can use to make the site more informative for your target audience? Also, do you have a logo or colour scheme that you want to see reflected in the site?

How often will the site be updated?
Are you planning on the website staying more or less the same over time, or will some content (for example news or updates about your company, or prices and product information) be updated on a regular basis?

Will there be online ordering on the site?
Think about your target audience when you make this decision. Will they really want to order online, or is the purchasing process more complex for them?

Will there be any other special features on the site?
Is there anything you can include that will appeal to your customers? For example, a calculator for making rough mortgage or tax calculations might be a useful tool on a site offering financial services. A painter might include a 'ready reckoner' calculator to allow visitors to figure out how much it would cost to paint a flat.

What are the best relevant competitor websites I have seen?

It's very helpful to find relevant sites whose style or functions appeal to you. What do you like about these sites – is it the design, the quality of the content, the easy ordering processes, or something else?

What other sites have I seen that might bring something relevant?

Don't just focus on your own sector – consider other sites that you like which may have something relevant to offer. Also check out sites that are frequently visited by your target audience and see what you can learn from them.

Starting simple

Even if you decide that your company will need to build a complex system with many features, it's best to consider building something simpler to start with. Designing the full system may take quite a long time, so you should have a strategy to launch something more straightforward at the outset and then gradually add more features as appropriate.

Many successful eBay sellers, for example, have only a very simple website, or no website at all. Equally, many car dealers have a successful online presence through a site such as *Auto Trader*, and it probably costs a lot less than it would to develop a site of their own.

Equally, many nightclubs and venues use a Facebook page to keep in touch with their regular clientele. It allows them to keep in touch with their online 'friends', and there is usually no expense involved. Facebook can also be used as a means to advertise to customers in your target customer demographics in your locality.

Dublin bar and night club Howl at the Moon uses its Facebook page to keep in touch with thousands of regular customers by answering their questions and letting them know about special offers and promotions.

Implementing your website project

Any website project consists of two main parts, known as the 'back end' and the 'front end'.

The **front end** is what the visitor to the website actually sees. It consists of the design, the graphics, the look and all the text that makes up the website.

The **back end** is the part that makes the site work, but which may not be directly visible to the visitor. It covers things like sending an e-mail through the site, searching the site, making an order, making a payment, editing account details, and many other aspects. It usually has to be linked into the processes and systems within your company.

Initial planning for the front end

If this is the first website you are developing, you will probably want to put most of your effort into the front end. Spend some time documenting what you would like to appear on the site and how you would like it to be presented.

Information architecture and user interface design

'Information architecture' is the process of structuring the information on your site. Think carefully about how you might organise your site's content into sensible sections, so that your target audience will be able to find the information they need: people have very little patience when they're looking for information online and if it's more than a few clicks away, they won't bother hanging about.

When you are designing a small site, the most important thing is to follow the conventions of Web design. There are some standard sections that almost all sites have, and you should have these too. The core sections that almost any website will have are:

- **Home Page.** The introduction to the site, with links to all the other sections. It usually includes a one-sentence statement of what the business is all about.
- **About Us.** This section describes the people and the organisation behind the company. It may contain information about the company's history, about the management, and about the people who work at the company. It may also have information about what makes the company unique.
- **Contact Us.** This section explains how to get in touch with your business. It may be a list of phone numbers, or it may have an e-mail form or other mechanism for getting in touch. It may also have your address and directions or maps to help your customers find their way to your office or shop. It's absolutely critical that this page works well.
- **Products or Services** (although these may be known by another name). This page contains the core information about what your company offers to the public.

Look at other sites, especially sites in your own sector, to see what the typical sections are.

Think about what special sections you might need. Do you want a blog – a constantly updated section of the site with your company's latest news or views? Some companies have a 'support' section to deal with customers' problems. Occasionally, sites have a 'forum' section.

At some point, you will need to prepare a simple 'site plan' which will indicate how the site will be structured. This site plan is a critical document, and you should ensure that it provides a place for all the information you will need to have on your website, and that it can be expanded reasonably easily if you need to add information, as you add new products and services, for example.

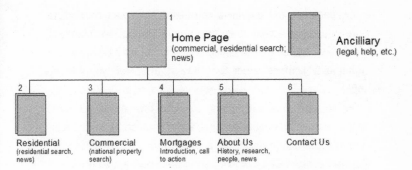

A basic site plan for an extensive website. Each page is numbered, so that it is easy to refer to individual ones. A double page indicates that this is the first page of a larger section which has a separate site map of its own.

User Interface Design, or UI design for short is something you will need to think about. UI design is the craft of making a website or computer program as easy to use as possible. If you already have a website, or want to evaluate a competitor's website, one good way to find out how well the UI has been designed is to ask a person who knows nothing about the site to try it out and to find some specific information. Watch carefully as the tester tries to find the information he or she is looking for – you may be surprised at the number of wrong turns the user will make. It's a good idea to perform at least basic testing of this type before launching any website. Jakob Nielsen's website on information architecture (**http://useit.com**) gives further details on how to conduct user testing.

The content

At this point you should have a clear idea of how large your website will actually be. Remember that if it contains more than a few pages, it will require a considerable amount of work to write sufficient material. Keep this in mind during your planning. It may be a better idea to concentrate on writing a few pages of high-quality content rather than having to spread yourself too thinly.

Decide who is actually going to write the content. It takes time to write good-quality material, and if you don't have the skills in-house, you may have to hire a writer from outside. Remember, too, that content which works well in print may not work so well online.

Have a clear plan of what content you want on your website. You could include graphics, text, data sheets and photos. A lot of the content may need to be written from scratch, although you may be able to repurpose material from sales material you have already.

The sooner you start putting this content together, the better. Start collecting relevant material right away. If there is content to write, start to sketch down the outline of the content in as much detail as you can. You may want to enlist the help of someone who has good writing skills in order to finish it off really well.

If you have time, do a keyword analysis for your website. To do this, think about all the words and terms that prospective customers might search for on Google or Yahoo! in order to find the products or services you provide. To compile this list of words and terms, engage the help of your staff and your friends, by asking them how they would use a search engine to look for your product or service.

Once you've determined these keywords, review your content plan and make sure these words are included. The search engines can only index the information they find on the site – they have no other way of directing appropriate customers to your site – so don't let this slide.

Producing high-quality text for your site

Getting your content plan together is a good start, but how can you use the content to make your website as easy to understand as possible?

Take a look at some of the best websites to see how they present their content.

One of the things that makes the website of Foxtons estate agents work well is that the title ('Foxtons: Estate Agents in London and Surrey') clearly states what the site is about, up-front, in clear terms. The short sentence underneath it (only 26 words) conveys the scale of the Foxtons operation, although perhaps it should say more about the types of property the company markets and the quality of the service.

Foxtons' website.

MAKING AN IMPACT ONLINE

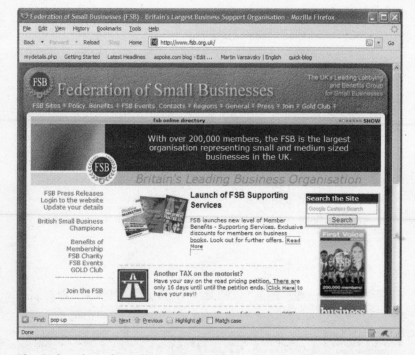

The Federation of Small Businesses has a clear headline that explains what the organisation is all about. The site is written in easy-to-understand language and directs visitors to the most relevant sections of the site.

Light Bulbs UK a site selling light bulbs, also states what the site is all about up-front. The left-hand navigation menu gives a clear guide to the categories of goods that are available. There is a telephone number clearly displayed twice for the benefit of people who feel uncomfortable ordering online.

Tips on writing for the Web

Gerry McGovern, a leading Web content specialist, has put forward the following pointers for writing effective web content:

1. **Know your reader. All effective writing begins with this. Write for your reader, not for your ego. Your reader is not everybody. The most effective writing is keenly focused on the specific needs of a clearly defined reader type. Is your reader a middle-class,**

female American, with two kids, who lives in the
suburbs?

2. **Take a publishing approach.** Publishing is about
getting the right content to the right person at the
right time at the right cost. It's about getting and
keeping attention with content. It's about driving
actions. Publishing is about selling with content.

3. **Keep content short and simple.** In publishing, less is
nearly always more. Remember, customers who are
scanning your site are impatient. Here are some
guidelines for the length of your content:
   - Headings: 8 words or less
   - Sentences: 15–20 words
   - Paragraphs: 40–70 words
   - Documents: 500 words or less

4. **Write active content.** The most powerful word in the
English language is 'YOU'. Write from the point of
view of the reader. Readers have come to your website
to do something, so your content should be written in
an action-orientated style. Every sentence needs to
move them towards a purchase, a subscription and a
solution.

5. **Put content in context.** The Web is about links and
connections. Web content is classified and linked
content. Never leave your reader at a dead-end on your
website.

6. **Write for how people search.** Write to be found when
people are searching. That means using the words your
target readership is using. Before you begin writing, sit
down and plan the keywords you will use in your
content. (For more details about this, see Chapter 3.)

7. Write great headings. Headings are the most important piece of content you will write. That's because:
   - People scan read and the first piece of content they often read is the heading. If it's not interesting, they're gone.
   - The heading is often used as title metadata. This is what the search engines use on the search results page. The heading may be placed on a home page as a link to the content.

   When you're writing headings:
   - Keep them to 8 words or less.
   - Make sure you include the most important keywords.
   - Cut out as many adjectives and articles (the, a, an) as possible.
   - Be clear and precise.
   - Avoid Shakespearean references (unless your audience will know them!).
   - Avoid being too clever: remember you're writing for your audience, not your ego.

8. Write excellent summaries. The summary is the 'who, what, where, when, how'. It's about getting the facts across in 50 words or less. An objective of a summary is to make people want to read on. Keep summaries punchy and factual.

9. Remember, people scan read. If the first sentence in the paragraph is not interesting, they'll move on. So, always lead off a paragraph with a factual sentence.

10. Write great metadata. If you can't write good metadata, you can't write for the Web. Metadata gives Web content context, so see it as an extension

of grammar. (In fact, you might say that it *is* Web grammar, in a sense.)

Classification (categorisation) is metadata. Focus on what classification terms are used on your website. It's your responsibility to ensure that your content is properly classified. Misclassified Web content might as well not have been written, because no one will be able to find it.

Headings and summaries are metadata. Date of publication and author information are metadata. Every Web page should have title metadata – a unique title that precisely describes the content on that page.

11. Edit. Edit. Edit. If at all possible, get someone else to edit your content: you become so close to text that you've written that you start agreeing with yourself, so someone else's viewpoint is ideal here. If you are editing someone else's content:

    take your time. Good editing can take anything from 30–50% of the time it took to write the original content.

    aim to do about three edits.

    edit first for style and tone. Ask these questions: Is it clear? Is it necessary? Is there a shorter way to say this? Is there a simpler way to say this?

    leave the checking of grammar and spelling until last. For a thorough edit, print out the content. Get a ruler. Place the ruler at the end of the content and read backwards.

(For full details, and to subscribe to Gerry McGovern's weekly newsletter, see: www.gerrymcgovern.com/)

Graphics

Your site should have a look and feel that you are happy with. Again, there is an array of choices. At the simplest, your site can have very simple graphics or none at all, or it can be designed according to a simple template. At the most complex, the site can have a very customised and distinctive look to fit with your identity. However, this will cost more and take longer to implement.

While it is, of course, beneficial to spend time and money on designing your website so that it looks good, you should always put the emphasis on making it simple to use. Some graphical add-ons are just gimmicks. For example, having a 'splash screen' animation which customers must watch before they access the main content of the site is unlikely to help make them feel comfortable on your site. Likewise, the navigation of the site needs to be clear. Look at the way the graphics are used on other sites that are relevant to your target audience.

Some of the key uses for graphics include:

Logos and corporate identity. If you have a logo, think about how it should be incorporated in your site. If you don't have a logo, seriously consider commissioning one as part of your website development.

Product shots and company shots. If possible, you should illustrate your website with pictures of the products you sell and, if appropriate, your company's facilities. Photographs make your site a lot more interesting, and may make it easier for your customers to understand exactly what you are offering. You may have good photographs already, or you may be able to get them from the manufacturers who supply you. If you use photographs from another source, make sure you get written permission to use them.

Video and animation. You might think that any type of video is going to be prohibitively expensive for your low-budget website. In fact, it may be possible to produce a very short video to illustrate some point about your product.

If so, you may be able to produce something simple yourself or with the help of friends, using inexpensive home recording equipment. Be prepared to spend a lot of time and some money to arrange this, especially if the video needs to have a really professional look.

Once you've produced your video, you can upload it to a video sharing website such as **YouTube** (**www.youtube.com**), and your Web designer can embed it into your website. This minimises the technical effort involved in storing the video online and serving it to users. Some people may also find your videos and your business through the **YouTube** site. (There are a number of alternative sites which provide a similar service, such as **vimeo.com.**)

You can also use a technologies like HTML5 and Flash to produce an animation that illustrates your product in context. Again, this doesn't come cheap and requires the expertise of a flash specialist, but the expense will be justified if it really serves to illustrate your product.

The possibilities that technology now offers to add multimedia features to your website are endless. However, do think hard about whether these features are genuinely going to add value to your business. Look at your competitors' sites and any sites you admire to get some ideas on how you can best use technologies to promote your business.

Plan for updates

Any website you launch is going to be just a starting point – there will be updates to it over the months and years following the launch. It is critical to decide how the content will be maintained and updated over time. If there is pricing information or other time-sensitive data on your site, you will certainly need to update it on a frequent basis.

If you plan on updating your website regularly with new content, you might consider having a blog instead of a website. There is more information on this below in the 'Blogging for business' section (see page 111), as well as in Chapter 2.

The back end

A major back-end development is not likely to be part of your plan if you are developing your first website ever, but the main back-end components you will want to consider are as follows:

- **contact forms.** Most sites have contact forms that can be used by site visitors to lodge queries. You can make it a requirement for customers to provide specific information (such as their phone number) when they are filling in the form. This makes it easier to get all the information you need from prospective customers so that you can give them a comprehensive reply as quickly as possible.
- **ordering system or shopping cart.** If your site is to sell products, you will need some type of ordering and payment system. Not only will you have to think about how to collect the order, you will also have to think about how your orders will be dealt with within your organisation.
- **content management system.** If you want to frequently update your site with news or new information, you will need some sort of content management system to allow you or your staff to make the changes. Otherwise you may have to go back to the Web designers every time there are changes to be made. A blog is one type of content management system which might be suitable for updating your site (see page 111).

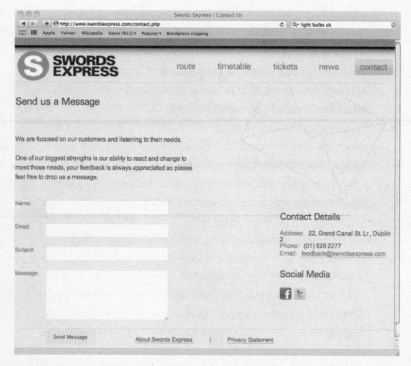

A typical contact form to allow customers to send a message to a company from a website. (www.swordsexpress.com).

That's just the basics. Back-end development can become far more complex as your website requirements grow. Further details on developing a complex Web application that integrates more comprehensively into your internal systems are given in Chapter 4.

If your requirements are fairly straightforward, there are inexpensive ways of building this back-end infrastructure. For example, Paypal provides a simple ordering and shopping cart system as part of its payment solution. See page 97 (E-commerce on a shoestring) for further details.

The basics of Web development

The core skills of Web development are quite straightforward. If you are developing something very simple or want to be able to do some basic maintenance work yourself, it's worth learning the basics. The main language of the Web is HTML (Hypertext Markup Language). HTML code looks like regular text, except that formatting is controlled by special tags which are used to indicate paragraph pages, links, images and so on. You will see some examples of HTML on the next few pages.

There are many software packages you can use to generate Web pages, and there may already be a suitable software package on your computer. For example, Front Page is part of the Microsoft Office Suite on Windows, and iWeb is part of the iLife suite on the Apple Macintosh. Many of these programs partly or fully hide the HTML code from you so you can edit pages almost as you would in a word processor. You may find that you still need to know some HTML to get the best out of these programs, though.

In order to demonstrate the basic techniques, we're going to work through an example of developing a Web page without any of these special tools. The example will show how you can edit the HTML directly, using a text editor such as Notepad.

Writing a simple HTML page

Start the Notepad program, which can be found in the Start All Programs Accessories menu in Microsoft Windows XP. (On a Macintosh, you can use SimpleText, which can be found in the Applications folder on the hard disk.) Then type:

```
<html>
<head>
<title>My first Web page!</title>
</head>
<body>
Welcome to our website.
</body>
</html>
```

As you can see, the HTML is basically regular text, interspersed with commands in angle brackets (< . . . >). These are called tags. Most tags are in pairs, with the second tag in the pair beginning with a forward slash (/). For example, the title of the page is surrounded by the <title> . . . </title> tags. The tags used in this example are the <title> . . . <title> tag, the <head> . . . </head> tags which enclose the introductory part of the page, the <body> . . .< /body> tag which encloses the main section of the page, and the <html> . . . </html> tag which identifies everything in between as HTML. Don't worry if you don't understand everything about these tags at this stage.

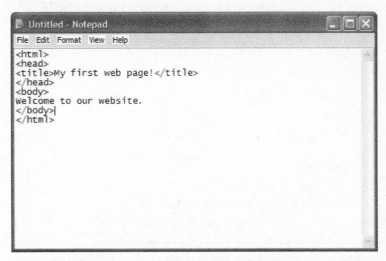

Screenshot of Notepad after typing a simple Web page.

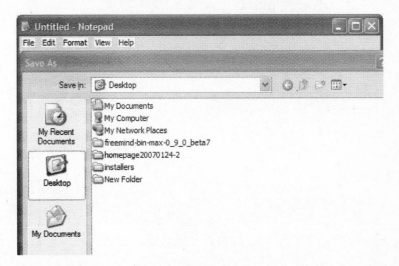

Now, save the file to your desktop (or another directory if you prefer).

Saving the HTML file to the desktop.

Now, check your desktop, and double-click on the testpage.html file. It will open in your Web browser.

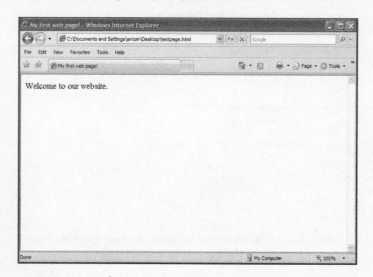

That's the basics. Now, you can add the details you want on your simple Web page. Open the file again, using Notepad. (If you cannot find the HTML file on the desktop when you go to open it, you may need to change the setting 'Files of type' to read 'All files').

Edit the file so that it reads as follows (substituting the details of your own business if you wish).

```
<html>
<head>
<title>Fred's Plumbers – plumbing and heating systems in
Dublin, Ireland</title>
</head>
<body>
<h1>Fred's Plumbers</h1>
<p>We are a small firm of plumbers. We work mainly on
domestic and small commercial installations. We can
install sinks and new boilers and hot tanks as well as
installing entire heating systems and bathrooms.
</p><p>
<a href=<0x201D>testpage.html">More about us</a>

<p>
22 Lr Grand Canal St
Dublin 2<br>
Ireland<br>
</p>
</body>
</html>
```

The file now contains a wider range of HTML 'tags', each of which is explained overleaf.

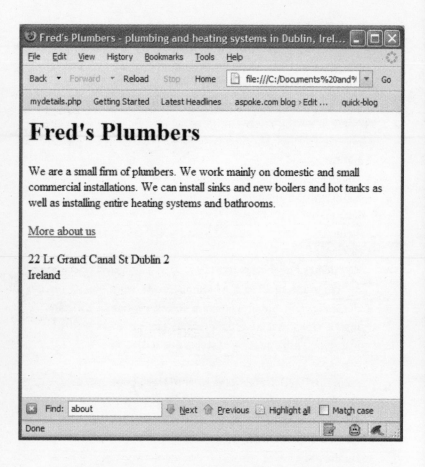

Save the file again, saving it as 'index.html', and open it as before by double-clicking on it. It will appear as follows:

<h1> ... </h1> means that any text between those codes is treated as a header.

<p> ... </p> treats the enclosed text as a paragraph.

 provides a line break

<a href=<0x201D>testpage.html<0x201D>>...</a> turns the enclosed text into a link, in this case to the 'testpage. html' page which we created earlier.

That's it! You've made a (very simple) Web page from scratch. It doesn't allow you to do much, but at least now you know the principles involved. Many professional Web designers code entire sites manually in this way.

There are numerous sites on the Internet where you can learn more HTML techniques.

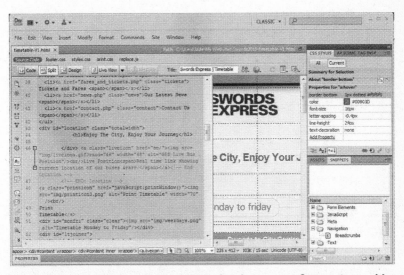

Dreamweaver is the best-known HTML development software. It provides sophisticated tools for a skilled web developer to develop complex, modern web pages.

Sites to check

Page Tutor (**www.pagetutor.com**) provides simple tutorials on developing basic but functional HTML pages. Another easy-to-follow tutorial on developing Web pages can be found at **www. w3schools.com/ html**

Uploading your pages

Once you've created your pages, using whatever tools you've chosen, publish them on your Web server. To access your website and upload the files, you will need the details that your hosting provider gave you.

The method shown here uses the 'My Network Places' tool built into Microsoft Windows. If you like, you can use other tools (such as CuteFTP on a PC, or using the 'Connect to Server' command in the Finder on a Macintosh).

First of all, you will need your FTP (file transfer protocol) settings, which will be provided by your hosting company. These include:

FTP User Name
This is the user name for your hosting account
FTP Password
This your password for your hosting account
FTP Site URL
ftp://www.yourdomainnamehere.com

Next, create a Windows XP Network Place, as follows.

1. **In Windows XP, select Start > My Network Places. In Windows 7, select Start > Computer. Then use the right mouse button to click on 'Computer' and select 'add network location'.**
2. **Under the 'Network Tasks' sidebar, select 'Add Network Place'. The 'Add Network Place' wizard page will be displayed.**

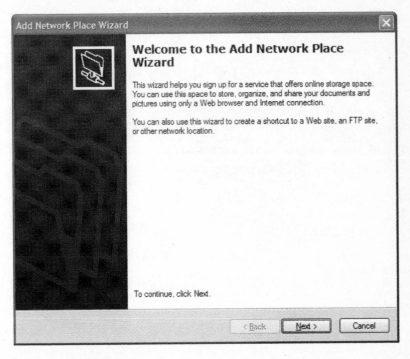

Click 'Next' to continue.

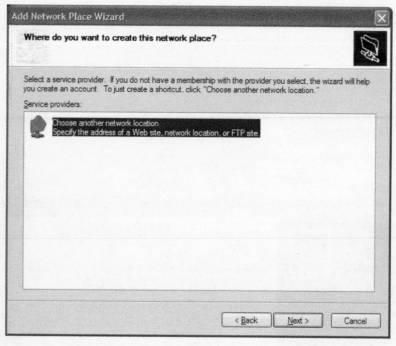

Click 'Next' to proceed to the next step.

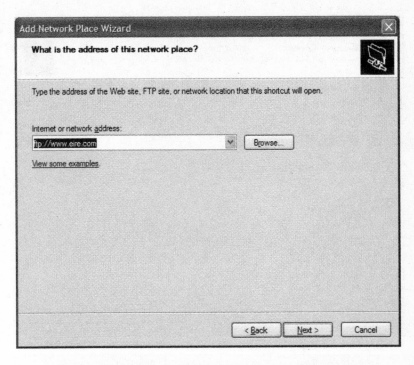

In the box for 'Internet or network address', type the FTP site name you were supplied with by the hosting company, preceded by the 'ftp://'. The example above is for the address 'www.eire.com'. Click 'Next' when you've typed the address correctly.

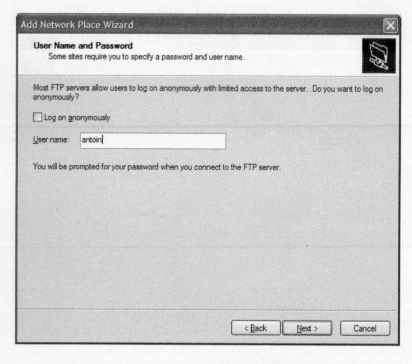

You will need to identify yourself in order to log in to make changes to your website. So untick 'Log in anonymously' and type in the username supplied to you by your hosting provider.

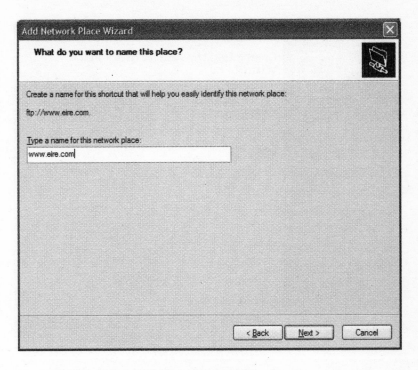

Just click 'Next' to set up the Network Place.

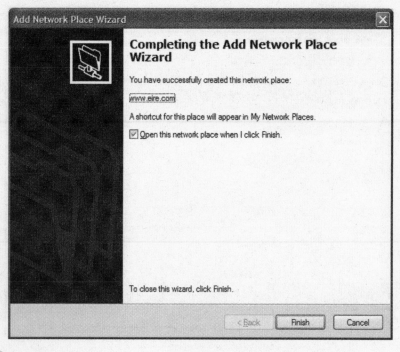

Now click 'Finish' and, providing you've done everything correctly, you'll see the following:

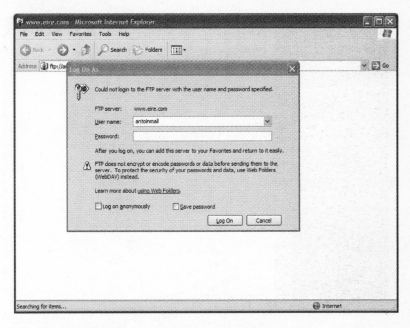

Type in the password supplied by your hosting provider, and click 'Log On'. Next, you'll see the following screen:

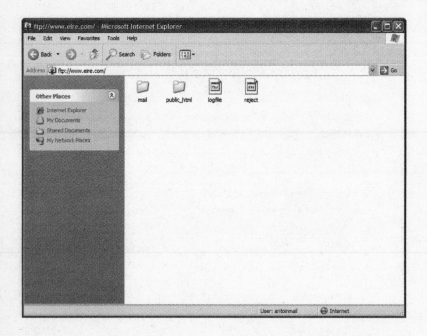

These are the files stored on your Web server. With this particular hosting provider, the pages for 'My website' need to be stored in the 'public_html' folder.

To transfer the files, simply copy the files on to the Web server in the same way you would copy files to any other folder on your computer, by using the copy and paste commands, or by dragging them from the desktop to the folder on the server.

Now, access your website at the address you have chosen, to check that your files have been correctly uploaded. If you have difficulties at this point you should contact the hosting company and ask them to talk you through the steps.

Content Management Systems

Updating websites by editing HTML and uploading directly to your website may be adequate if you hardly ever update your website. However, if you want to add new information or make edits on a regular basis, you will want a much more streamlined system.

Content management systems provide a simple, web-based means of editing and updating your website. New pages can be added and updates can be made through a web-based form.

There are many different content management systems with many different levels of complexity, depending on your requirements. Wordpress is shown here, which is adequate for many small business needs. If you have more sophisticated needs, for example, to allow for multi-lingual sites or complex layouts, you could consider the likes of Joomla and Drupal.

Wordpress is an example of a content management system which a web developer can configure to meet your exact needs. If you want to experiment with Wordpress, you can visit www.wordpress.com and create a 'blog' for free. However, if you want to actually use the website commercially, it is recommended that you use a paid-for service and get a domain name of your own.

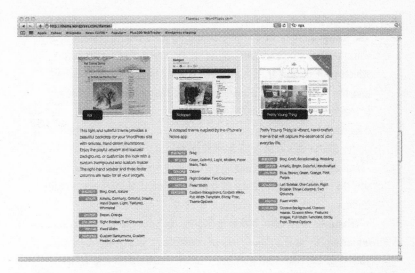

A content management 'theme' is the layout and styling which gives a website its unique look and feel. Libraries of existing themes are available, and your developer can base the look of your website on these.

E-commerce on a shoestring

Not every good commercial website needs to have an e-commerce aspect. Your product or service may not lend themselves to being sold through the online channel, for many reasons. There are a surprising number of areas, though, where online commerce can be a viable business, or provide a workable extension to an existing business.

At the simplest, you must have two things to be able to take orders online:

- **a way to take and record orders**
- **a means of payment**

Taking and recording orders

The most common way of implementing an ordering system is by using a 'shopping cart'. An online shopping cart records the items which your customer is interested in and the quantities required, and then allows the customer to finalise their order and get ready to pay for it. This is similar to a shopper in a supermarket, who chooses items from an aisle and places the items in a trolley, before going to the checkout with their final selections.

Not all sites need a shopping cart. It may not be appropriate for a site that sells custom items, or one that almost always sells single items.

Whatever way your ordering works on your site, it is equally important to have a robust way of managing the orders you receive. You need to make sure that every order is dealt with and correctly dispatched. Accurate and timely dispatch of goods is critical to a successful e-commerce enterprise.

Receiving payments online

Payment will depend on the type of business you operate. If you operate exclusively as a wholesaler with regular customers, for example, you will probably find that your payments need to be conducted through your current invoicing system, rather than through a direct online payment.

While this means you don't have to set up any new payment systems, orders from your website will have to be handled in such a way as to ensure that all items are correctly invoiced through your current accounting system. You will also have to decide whether to accept new customers through your website, and how accounts will be set up for them.

Doing business in foreign countries

One of the advantages of doing business on the Internet is the ease with which sales can be made to foreign countries where you would not normally have an opportunity to do business. If the products you are offering are attractive, you can expect to get enquiries from potential overseas purchasers. These marketplaces could well be lucrative for your company – they may be less competitive than your own marketplace. However, there are clear hazards to doing business internationally. You probably won't know the people involved as well as you know local operators, and if you don't get your payment, you have no easy way to pursue the matter, either in person or through the courts.

There is also extra paperwork to deal with. If you are inside the European Union and are shipping to another EU country, then the bureaucracy is minimal. However, if you are shipping beyond the EU borders, be aware that your customers will probably have to pay import duties and get the goods cleared through customs. This should be the customers' responsibility, and it's important to make it clear that the burden of these costs will fall to them. Even within the EU it is important to understand the rules about VAT when selling to other countries in the EU.

There are also a number of well-known scams on the Internet involving foreign trade. One common one is where a new customer gets in touch and offers to buy a large quantity of items at a good price, and promises to send a bank draft in payment. The draft duly arrives, but is for an amount larger than originally negotiated. The new customer asks the seller to send the extra cash back to him, either by way of a further bank draft, or via Western Union. It is only a few days later that it transpires that the bank draft is completely fake.

For all these reasons, it makes sense to be extremely careful when you do business outside your own country for the first time. While there are good customers out there, caution is required in dealing with them. You need to receive payment up-front, and you need to be sure that the payment is cleared before you ship any goods or incur expenses.

About the credit-card system

If you are selling mainly to the public, or to people outside your country, you will almost certainly want to accept payments by credit card. Although there have been many promises of new systems for paying for items online, credit cards are still by far the most popular option for Internet transactions.

Credit cards as we know them have been around since the 1960s, and were based on earlier systems designed for payment for fuel and other goods. Although there is now a lot more technology and security involved, the basic workings of the system have not changed all that much.

In any transaction, there are generally four different parties involved. Most importantly, there is the merchant, who is selling the goods or services, and the cardholder, who is making the purchase. The cardholder has had the card issued to them from their bank, called the 'issuer'. The merchant also has an arrangement with his bank, which is called the 'acquirer'. Both the issuer and the acquirer are affiliated to the international Card Association, which is responsible for coordinating the whole system. There are separate Card Associations for each of the credit-card brands (MasterCard, Visa and so on).

When the cardholder makes a purchase, she agrees to pay by credit card. This agreement can be made by signing or by keying in a PIN (personal identification number). Many merchants and acquirers allow the consent to be given orally over the phone or electronically via the Internet. Regardless of the means, the basic process is the same.

Electronic verification systems allow merchants to check whether the card is known to be stolen or lost, and whether there is sufficient credit available on the account. Additional information, such as the security code on the signature strip of the card, may be required to complete the verification. Once the merchant receives verification, he or she will go ahead and deliver the goods and services.

The issuer then pays the acquirer the amount due. This may happen within a day, or may take several weeks, depending on the particular situation. The acquirer then pays the merchant the amount due minus the commission, and the issuer includes the amount in the monthly bill to the cardholder. The cardholder pays at his or her convenience, and may avail of the credit facility to defer payment for several months or longer.

Every so often, a payment is disputed. This means that the cardholder has complained that a particular transaction is incorrect. They may claim that they never bought the goods or services at all, or that the goods or services were never delivered, or were of unacceptable quality. The acquiring and issuing banks will investigate to determine the issue. Where there is a dispute about whether the items were actually ordered, the banks will generally accept the word of the merchant if the cardholder paid using a PIN, or where a signature authorising the transaction is on file. However, where the cardholder was not present to give a signature or enter a PIN, the banks will often decide in favour of the customer. Where this happens, the merchant will suffer a 'chargeback', meaning that the original amount will be deducted from his next payment from the issuing bank.

Generally speaking, the merchant has to carry the risk for chargebacks for Internet transactions. A certain proportion of transactions can be expected to be fraudulent if you are selling high-value, desirable items, and this has to be taken into account in planning your online business, particularly if you are trading overseas.

The acquiring bank also assumes some risk. If an e-commerce company collapses and, as a result, fails to deliver goods that have been ordered, the bank will have to carry the cost of refunding these charges, without any prospect of recovering this money from the merchant. This is the reason why many merchants have been reluctant in the past to provide credit-card acquiring services to new online businesses. They now commonly take precautions such as only paying out to new merchants four weeks or longer after a transaction has gone through.

Setting up an online shop with Paypal

Although there are many technicalities involved in setting up an e-commerce site, a number of companies have devised systems that make it much easier to accept orders and sell goods online. These may not be the long-term answer for your e-commerce needs, but they give you an opportunity to experiment with developing an e-commerce system without any major capital outlay.

The biggest and best-known company of this type is Paypal, a subsidiary of eBay. eBay bought Paypal in order to provide a solid payment system to underpin its auction business. You can use Paypal on your own site, without having to sell through eBay.

The first step to accepting payments is to register with Paypal and set up an account. Go to the Paypal home page (**www.paypal. com**), and follow the link for Merchant Services. You will need to sign up for a business account.

Once you have done that, you may have to wait a short period (usually a few days) for your account to be approved. It may also be necessary to verify your account using a credit card. Once it is approved, you can set up your online shop.

Setting up a 'Buy Now' button

The simplest way of selling goods on Paypal is to set up a 'Buy Now' button to place on your website. This button has all the information about the name and price of your product embedded in it. When a customer clicks on it, they are taken to the Paypal site and asked to make a payment using a credit card or a Paypal account, if they have one.

Setting up a Paypal 'Buy Now' button is quite simple. However, you will need basic HTML skills to implement it, and so you may need the help of your Web developer. He or she will be able to follow the instructions and incorporate the Paypal HTML button into your HTML.

The first step is to log into your Paypal account and go to 'Merchant Tools'. If you have the time, read the various tutorials on the site, so that you can better understand how Paypal works and discover the other options that the company offers for small businesses. Then find the option 'Buy Now' button. (You may have to search around to find this.) It will lead you to a form similar to the page below.

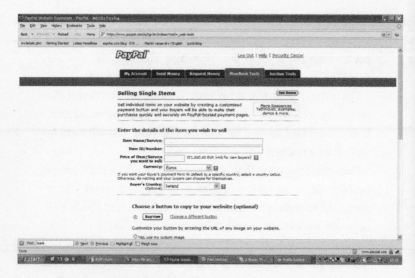

Simply enter a description of the item you are selling.

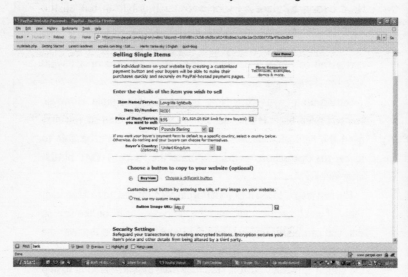

And click 'Create Button Now' at the bottom of the page.

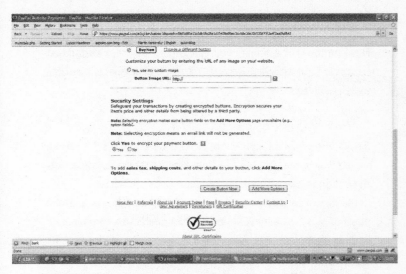

Paypal will then return you a page containing a snippet of HTML code. This is the code that you or your Web developer will need to incorporate into your Web page.

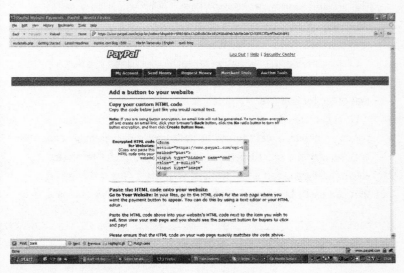

Of course, this is only the simplest payment mechanism that Paypal can offer. There are many other options for setting up your 'Buy Now' button. For example, you can choose to use a customised button to fit in with your website. Your Web developer will be able to help with this.

Setting up a shopping cart with Paypal

Paypal also offers a simple shopping cart system. You set it up in a similar way to the 'Buy Now' button, except that the customer gets the option to buy a number of products in one purchase.

The Paypal shopping cart does have limitations, however, and it may not be suitable for your needs. If you prefer, you can integrate another shopping cart system from a third-party vendor to work with Paypal. You should discuss the cost and complexity of doing this with your Web developer.

Receiving payments and viewing orders in Paypal

The 'account overview' function in Paypal offers you an easy way to view your orders. You can see orders as they arrive and also view your current balance at a glance.

Clicking on the 'details' option for each order allows you to see it in its entirety, so that you can see all the items that were included in that order, for example.

What's more, the site gives you the option to print out a packing slip which you can use to track your order internally and enclose with the order when you ship it. If you prefer to process electronically, you can also download your latest orders in a format that can easily be opened in Microsoft Excel or another database program.

Withdrawing funds

You can withdraw your funds from your Paypal account to any ordinary bank account. Simply go to the withdraw tab. The first time you withdraw from a particular account, you will need to add it to the system by keying in the account name, number and other details. The next time, the money can be withdrawn with a few clicks.

Disputes with Paypal

Occasionally, a dispute will arise regarding a Paypal transaction. You will need to deal with it through the Resolution Centre. The process is as follows.

If a customer is unhappy – because an item has not been delivered, for example – they will raise a 'Dispute' on Paypal. You will receive an e-mail informing you of the problem, and you will need to deal with it through the 'Resolution Centre' function of the Paypal site. The customer may also escalate the Dispute into a complaint. If this happens, you will generally be expected to provide proof of delivery or to give a refund to the customer. Paypal will adjudicate on the case if there is no resolution. If the seller is unable to provide proof of delivery, there is a high probability that the adjudication will go against the seller.

Staying the right side of your payment provider

One of Paypal's strengths is that it enables small businesses to easily accept credit cards and do business on the Internet, and therefore allows them to compete on a bit more of an even footing than they'd have normally with much bigger competitors. Paypal lets you get into business with a minimum of bureaucracy and paperwork. Most small businesses never have a problem with Paypal, and find it to be a good service at a reasonable price.

However, if you get on the wrong side of Paypal or any other payment provider, you may find yourself in a difficult spot. Paypal takes a dim view of anyone whom it believes may have tried to abuse its systems, and understandably so. It will take action to ban any abuser and may freeze the account. Critics say, however, that Paypal sometimes acts arbitrarily, without any good reason and that it is difficult to appeal a decision to restrict an account.

Tips for dealing with Paypal (or other payment providers)

■ Do read the Paypal terms and conditions. There are many rules that you may not aware of. For example, you may not do transactions over the phone and enter them into your Web ordering system, and you may not have more than one Paypal account for a person or business. Also, certain types of products and services (mainly gambling and adult products) cannot be sold through Paypal.

■ Keep your account balance low. Move the money out of the Paypal account as soon as you have accumulated a few hundred pounds in income.

■ Keep an eye on your account for disputes and complaints. It is important to resolve these as rapidly as possible.

■ Watch out for 'phishing' attempts. Phishing is sending false e-mails in order to try to get a user to reveal their username and password details, thinking that they are logging into a legitimate site. The only way you should ever log on to the Paypal site is by typing in the Web address and keying in your username and password manually.

■ Have a solid password and take good care of it. Make sure that your password has both numbers and letters in it and that is really hard to guess. Also, don't give out your password, even to your Web developer. If it's necessary for multiple users to be able to access your account, Paypal has a special multi-user feature to facilitate this in a secure way.

Google Checkout

Google offers an alternative to PayPal for sellers in the US and the UK. It is worth considering as an alternative or as an additional means of payment. Like with PayPal, you only pay a commission on what you sell and there is no up-front charge.

Other payment services

There are a number of other payment services, which offer broadly similar services to Paypal. The best-known international players are **2checkout.com** and **worldpay.com**. Another option is to work with your existing bank, who will put you in touch with a payments processor, such as Realex (**www.realex.ie**) who will handle the integration of the service.

Although these systems are not as easy to set up as the one provided by Paypal, they all offer the same basic functionality, such as the acceptance of credit-card and other payments. They will cost you more time and money to implement than Paypal, however, because of the extra paperwork that is generally involved, and the more complex integration work needed. Your Web developer may need to bring in different skills in order to integrate them.

When choosing an acquirer or payment service, whether it is with Paypal or with a payment provider like Worldpay, or through your own bank, it's important to consider the following issues:

- **set-up costs.** Most acquirers will have an up-front charge which you must pay before you go into business.
- **ease of integration.** How much work will be involved in getting your Web developer to get it to work with your site? The acquirer should be able to give you some documentation to allow you to evaluate this.

- **commission.** The acquirer makes money by charging you a commission which is a percentage of the amount you are paid. Obviously, the lower the commission, the better. It is also preferable if commission is on a sliding scale, so that as you sell more goods, your commission goes down. Beware that some acquirers charge a minimum fee per transaction. If you do a lot of small-value transactions, this may be a significant cost for you.
- **payment schedules.** Some acquirers will give you access to your funds almost immediately; others will take two weeks or longer.
- **reputation and relationship.** It's better to deal with an acquirer with whom you already have a direct relationship, such as the bank where you have your business account. This makes it easier to resolve any problems that arise.

Don't be afraid to start with one service, to keep costs down, and then to switch to another as you become successful. The important thing in the early stages is to get up and running and test your concept and marketing plans. You can fine-tune the business processes and the cost model later on.

Blogging for business

A 'blog' or 'weblog' is a section of a site that is updated with news or other content on a regular basis, usually on a daily or weekly basis. There are many benefits to having a weblog on your site:

- **it's low cost.** A blog is a cheap way to get your message out on a regular basis. The main investment is the time taken to prepare the material.

- **it gives your site a personality.** Many small business sites are drab and boring, nothing like the colourful businesses that lie behind them. Blogs allow the interest and the enthusiasm to bubble though.
- **it gives people a reason to return to your site.** Customers love to return to a site that will have something new and interesting.
- **it helps your search-engine rankings.** Regularly updated content, containing plenty of relevant keywords, will help you appear with a higher ranking on search engines like Google.
- **it gives customer feedback.** It allows customers and others to give you feedback and establish a dialogue with your company.

The blogs below are good examples of dynamic, regularly updated blogs run by small businesses, with few resources except for their writers' enthusiasm.

However, producing an interesting weblog requires an investment of valuable time. If you decide to get one up and running, be sure that you'll be in a position to add new content to it at least once a week or so.

Innocent, the smoothies and juices company, updates its blog a few times a week. The regularly updated content brings repeat traffic to the site from consumers and from people in the trade.
(See http://innocentdrinks.typepad.com)

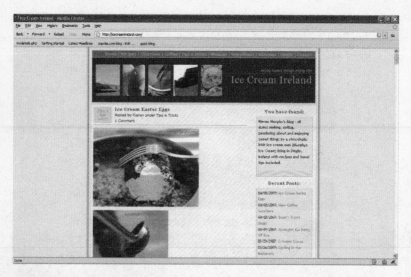

Murphy's Ice Cream, a much smaller company based in Kerry in Ireland, gets its message out through a weblog maintained by the owner, Kieran Murphy. It gives the company and its product a personal appeal. (See http://icecreamireland.com)

Blogging Software

Blogging software is a type of content management software geared specifically towards content that is frequently updated. The most popular software for blogging is Wordpress (www.wordpress.com and www.wordpress.org) which has already been mentioned in the section above.

Facebook

Facebook is a social networking site with over 500 million active users worldwide and 26 million in the UK, so there is a good chance that many of your customers are on Facebook.

You can set up a Facebook page for your business. Customers or others who are interested in your content can choose to affiliate themselves to you by clicking the 'like' button on your Facebook page.

You can then update your Facebook page, a little as you might update a blog, and other people can then comment on what you say or on your company generally. However, Facebook entries are usually shorter and snappier than the typical blog entry.

A Facebook page for a small business, incorporating updates, comments and other information.

Twitter

Twitter is a social networking site where the emphasis is on conversation and back-and-forth dialogue. Twitter has around 175 million users worldwide, and around 6 million of those are thought to be in the UK.

Twitter page for Kieran Murphy, who operates Murphy's Ice Cream, an ice cream maker and retailer in Dingle, Co. Kerry.

LinkedIn

LinkedIn is a more targeted, niche player in social networking. Rather than spreading itself over the whole consumer spectrum, it focuses on professional and corporate uses. It is the most serious and most formal of the social networking sites. A typical LinkedIn profile reads like a resumé or curriculum vitae. LinkedIn's main income is from recruitment advertising and business-related services.

117

A typical LinkedIn profile.

Next step

Once you've built a good website, the most important part of any online sales strategy in the early stage is to get exposure to your marketplace. A strong marketing plan and good implementation is essential for success. The next chapter explains the key issues for getting your company name out there and attracting the right kind of traffic to your site.

3 MARKETING YOUR WEBSITE

> A site that isn't marketed and isn't visited by prospective customers might as well not exist, no matter how good it is. It's critical that you work out an objective for the type of traffic you want, and a strategy to get the traffic you need.

Have a clear objective

Be clear about what you want to achieve online before you start investing time and money in marketing your site. You may have simple ambitions to start with; you want to put your business on the site and ensure that your current customers can find it easily. You will be concentrating on the same market as before, and your website will be a supplement to your existing sales and marketing efforts, rather than a replacement.

Although it is not essential, you can still benefit from some carefully targeted online promotion. Think about how customers might find your business through the Internet, and take some basic steps to make sure they do. Also, think about customer service on the Internet – what will happen when a query comes in to the site?

You may also benefit from using the Internet as a tool to keep in contact with your existing customers. For many small and medium-sized businesses, this might be the most important part of your Internet communications strategy. If you can stay in touch with existing customers and keep them informed about your company and your products, they are more likely to remain loyal customers and refer other business to you.

An Internet-oriented business

You may envisage the Internet playing a broader role in your business in the future. If you regard it as a primary channel to attract new customers and to orient part of your business around the needs of Internet users, it's important that customers are able to find you easily when they search on the Internet for your services or products. Then, when they find you, your website will have to impress them and hold their attention long enough to encourage them to call you or place an order. So think about who your online audience will be, and how you can serve their needs.

Your audience

In Chapter 2, you've already thought about how your target audience might interact with your website; now it's important to consider how this audience typically uses the Internet: how can they find out about your site and come and do business with you?

It is critical that you clearly identify the audience that you wish to attract to your site. If you do not have a clear objective, you may find that you are attracting the wrong kind of traffic.

Product and positioning

With a target audience in mind, review your products or services and the way you position them. What works well in person with your existing base of customers may not be as clear and well defined to your target market on the Internet. It may make sense to concentrate on certain types of product or service when you promote on the Internet.

Concentrate on your strengths

If you plan on using the Internet as a primary channel, one option might be to concentrate on a small number of products that are likely to be of interest to your Internet customers. There is little point in offering goods on your website that are already available in shops everywhere and on many other websites. You will have more success if you focus on some niche where you can be a market leader and where your expertise and more personal touch can attract customers. For example, an electrical retailer might want to concentrate on environmentally friendly, low-energy products.

Communicate your positioning clearly

As well as picking the right product or service to sell on the Internet, you have to make sure that you communicate it in a way that makes sense to your target audience and which will entice them to buy the product from you. For example, if you want to extend your electrical goods business online, you might decide to concentrate on some specific type of product (say, coffee makers or food processors) and provide more information and a more personal and expert service than is available in a local shop.

This is your 'positioning'. Although you are offering the same product as the local shop, you are positioning yourself differently in the marketplace, to appeal to customers who want detailed, expert information about products before buying.

Even if your business isn't going to be completely Internet-based, it's still important that you carefully consider your positioning. For example, if plumbers want to put information about their services on the Internet, they should think about the reasons why people might search on the Internet for a plumber in their area. On the one hand, they might want to install a new bathroom and be looking for quotations; on the other, they might be looking for help on an emergency basis to fix a leaking pipe or a blocked drain.

Although plumbers might currently carry out both types of service for their regular customers, they need to determine how to 'position' the business for the future when designing a website – whether to concentrate on one type of work or the other, or to follow some middle path.

The key is to find a way to differentiate yourself that will be appealing to your target audience and profitable for your own business.

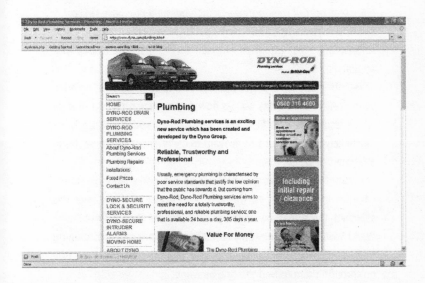

Dyno-rod, which operates a plumbing franchise, has a clear positioning – their franchisees are completely focused on emergency drain repair work, not on new installations.

Strategies to promote your website online

Once your objectives are clear, and you have considered whether the product and positioning you have is correct for your target audience, you need to consider the exact means by which you will drive your traffic.

Increasing your prominence in Web search engines like Google and Yahoo!

Search engines are the way in which most people find products and services on the Internet. Research by Harris Interactive and iCrossing in the US indicates that 67% of adults use a search engine as part of their online research before a purchase (**http://searchmarketing.yahoo.com/srch/keystats. php**). Not surprisingly, most attention is given to the first few results that appear.

You obviously want to get your site to appear as close as possible to the top of the results list. So how do the search engines decide which results to show first? They try to figure out which pages are most likely to be useful and relevant to users. They determine this in a number of ways.

Firstly, they look at the content of the page, and determine whether it is relevant to the Web user's search. If the user has searched for something very specific (maybe for 'cfl light bulbs Wandsworth'), there may only be 10 or so relevant pages containing these words. These will all be displayed, and the customer can easily go through them to find the one he wants.

However, many searches on the Internet are much less specific: for example, a user might search simply for 'light bulbs'. There are millions of pages on the Internet containing this term, and it will only be possible to show a small proportion of them. The search engine has to prioritise the massive list of pages that might be relevant.

Most search engines use the following criteria to determine how high to show a particular site on the results listing:

- **are there a lot of links to that page or to the site it contains?** The more links to the page, the more trusted and authoritative the page is considered to be.
- **is the link text that is used to link to that page relevant to the current search?** The link text is the text that is highlighted and which the user clicks on to reach the page.
- **how much traffic does that site receive?** Some search engines have access to statistical information about site traffic. It is assumed that busier sites might be better than less used ones.
- **is the site geographically relevant?** If you search on the **google.co.uk** site, for example, the results tend to be biased towards UK sites rather than US sites and you can even exclude non-UK sites completely.

There are a number of small but significant ways in which you can make your search engine more likely to be comprehensively indexed by Google, Yahoo! and other search engines. Using these techniques can make a big difference to where you appear in the search-engine rankings. This process is known as 'search-engine optimisation'. The basic techniques are as follows.

Keyword analysis

Identify the keywords by which you want to be found. Take a sheet of paper and write down the words and phrases that a customer is likely to type into a search engine to find your company. Typically, this will include:

- the name of your sector
- the town you are located in
- the types of products you make or sell or the services you provide
- the brand names under which your products are sold
- competitors' brand names (although it is important that you do not suggest incorrectly that you are linked to that competitor)
- related sectors

Remember to think about how your audience will search for your products or services, as well as how you refer to the product in your trade or business. A householder looking for a plumber, for instance, will most likely search for 'new bathroom' or 'drain clearing' rather than for 'plumber' or 'tradesman'.

Pick the most important of these words and make sure they are used in the site. If the words aren't present, the search engine won't pick up on them and searchers won't be directed to your site.

Have the right keywords, in the right place on your site

Your keywords should occur as part of the text of your site. It is particularly important that they are featured prominently in the title of the page (which usually appears for users as part of the header bar of the browser, rather than within the browser itself) and in the headings on the page. If possible, your Web developer should ensure that <H1> and <H2> tags are used on these headings. Research has shown that information in the titles and headings are given extra weight by search engines (see **http:// blog.v7n.com/2006/03/29/seo-copywriting**)

You may also want to get your developer to set the special meta keywords and description tags to provide extra information to the search engine. However, the usefulness of meta-tags nowadays is questionable; they are frequently abused, and many of the search engines now ignore them.

Make sure your keywords also appear in the first sentence or two of the body text on your home page. Equally, on subsequent pages, the most important information should be near the beginning of the page. This is for three reasons. Firstly, it is crucial to give visitors the key information they need as early as possible when they reach your site. Secondly, it ensures that these words are indexed by the search engine (some search engines only index the first portion of a very long page). Thirdly, some search engines use the first text from the page as the summary information that appears under the title of your site in the search result. This may be a valuable guide to customers.

Make sure your site has text links to all the pages that you want the search engine to link to. If the only way to get to a page is through a pull-down menu or a search system, those pages won't be indexed, and you won't get any links to them in search engines. Your Web developer can add a site map or make other changes to ensure that there are links to every page.

Equally, if there are dynamic pages on your website (i.e. pages that are automatically produced from a database rather than being written directly in HTML), some search engines may not add them to the index. You will need to ask your Web developer to remedy this problem, by making dynamically generated pages appear as static pages. To get the most from dynamically created pages:

■ avoid the use of the **?**, **%** and **&** symbols in pages' Web addresses. These symbols all indicate to the search engine that the page is dynamic, and it may avoid searching them as a result.

■ if you must use these symbols, keep the length of the Web address as short as possible.

■ be sure to have a link to every page of the website. If necessary, ask your Web developer to construct an automatically updated site map with links to all the dynamic pages.

For more details on these issues, see Marketing Experiments Journal – 'Dynamic Web Pages Tested' (**www.marketingexperiments. com/ ppc-seo-optimization/ dynamic-web-pages-tested. html)**

If you have several lines of business in your company (for example, different kinds of products or a variety of services), you could have a page for each major area and attempt to optimise that for the Internet rather than trying to optimise only the home page.

Many small companies want to focus their energies on a particular town or region. Make sure you include your address and details of the areas you serve on your website. It's a good idea to put your full address, including the postcode and the country, in the footer on every page in the site. This makes it more likely that your site will turn up for customers that search for a particular place name or postcode.

Search engine submission

To get found by the search engines, you need to submit your Web addresses to them, and they will have forms that will allow you to do that. Do not expect this to have much of a result, though. It will only make a difference if your site is completely new, or the particular search engine has never come across your site before. (If your site is linked from any other site, the search engines will probably find it anyway.)

Getting other sites to link to you

Page optimisation (improving the use of keywords) alone is not enough to get your website to appear high up in the search engines, particularly if there are a lot of competing sites. Where there are a number of websites with similar keywords, the search engines will usually rank them in terms of 'link popularity'. A site's link popularity basically depends on how many other sites link to it. More popular, authoritative sites are generally given more weight than small sites when calculating link popularity.

The best way to get page links is by producing very good content that people are interested in and that is 'linked to' frequently by other websites. The following are some typical ways to present this great content.

- Have articles published on other websites, and make sure that your Web address appears with the article. As well as providing links for search engines, this is a good way of building a profile for yourself and your business. Writing these articles does take time and effort, but can provide valuable rewards.
- have a blog, hosted on your own domain name, on which you post interesting and current content. If the content is good and up to date, you can attract others to link to you. Again, the benefits of having a blog go beyond just appearing in search engines. If you have a blog hosted on another domain name, you can help improve your page ranking by writing occasional stories about your company.

- **issue regular press releases with news about your business on your site, and follow up by submitting the releases to industry or local websites. If your news is interesting and well presented, you will attract at least some links. News on a website also gives the site a fresh look.**

These strategies can also be pursued more aggressively. If you can convince a journalist to write a story for a major newspaper with a website, and to include a link to your site in the story, that will have a significant impact on your link popularity. Another strategy is to court controversy – if you use your website or blog to put forward contentious views, it is far more likely to attract links and visitors. While this is a good way to build link popularity, it won't necessarily be good for your business, though.

There are a variety of tools and services available on the market to help you to optimise your website further. Do use these tools with care, thought, and avoid trying to fool the search engines into giving you an incorrect ranking or associating incorrect keywords with your Web pages. Some techniques may even result in your site being blacklisted. The website of a major international car manufacturer was completely removed from the Google search engine for a while, because it extensively used the controversial 'doorway' technique, where search engines are presented with a different version of the home page from the standard one shown to visitors. 'Link farming', a technique where you can buy links on a 'farm' of websites in order to artificially drive up your link popularity is no longer effective, because of adjustments that have been made to the major search engines.

The whole area of search engine optimisation will continue to evolve. If search-engine rankings are important to you, it would certainly be worth you getting hold of the tools and advice you need to improve your performance. However, make sure you are aware of exactly what is being done to promote your site and that it does not fall foul of the search engines' regulations (for further information on this, see **www.wilsonweb.com/ articles/ checklist.htm**).

Building a site map

A Web designer will be able to advise you on building a Google site map. This is a special file in a machine-readable format which makes it more likely that all the pages on your site will be properly indexed.

It's a good idea to subscribe to the Webmaster programs of the various search engines, particularly Yahoo! and Google. These tools will give you clues as to how often your site is being indexed, and whether all pages in your site are being visited (see **www.google. com/ webmasters/ sitemaps/ login**).

It is better to use text rather than images on your website, especially for important content such as names or links. Search engines cannot read text that is contained in images. If you must use images, be sure to include appropriate alternative text, using ALT tags (these provide descriptions of images). This text will be visible to the search engine.

Social Networking

Social networking sites provide an opportunity to continuously promote to existing customers. If you can, get existing customers to endorse your Facebook page by pressing 'Like'. This 'Like' button will appear on your Facebook page, but you can also have it appear on your main website. Once they've used the 'Like' button, you have an ongoing connection with these customers, via Facebook.

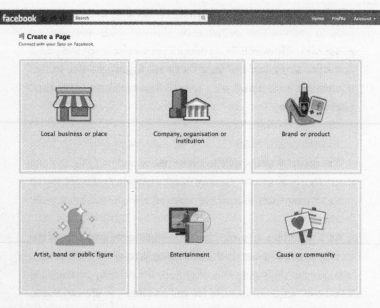

Facebook makes it fairly easy to create a Facebook page for your business. There is a link to the 'Create a page' function at the bottom of your Facebook profile page.

Equally, you can attract Twitter followers, who will then get regular updates from your company. You can also go further, by getting your customers and followers on Twitter and Facebook to repost the information you provide. On Facebook this is called 'sharing' and on Twitter this is called 'retweeting' or 'RTing'. For this to happen, you obviously have to produce content that is compelling and that your customers will consider worthwhile sharing with their friends.

Typical examples of ways to promote by these means are

- special offers which are time-limited (for example, a coffee shop could offer a free cup of coffee with any cake on a slow day.
- events and news which are likely to be of interest to the community (for example, a book launch by an author or an interesting story about how your business worked with a customer
- a link or other information which is funny or entertaining in its own right, like an explanatory video or a funny story. For you to get a benefit from this sort of exposure, the material obviously has to have a link to your business (see the section on viral marketing below).

If you can get them to work for you in even a small way, social networking sites are a great boon to your business. Facebook and Twitter do not charge you anything for their regular services, so there is little or no financial outlay, although you do have to consider the time you invest in them.

One long-term drawback of these sites could be that your relationships are mediated by the sites. You may find yourself dependent upon it to keep in regular touch with your customers, and a charge may eventually be imposed. If your online contacts are a very valuable part of your business, it is worth having an alternative means of electronic contact, for example by constructing a database of email addresses.

Other strategies

Search engines are not the only way to get relevant traffic to your site. There are many other useful techniques.

Give away something for free

If you can become the definitive source for information on some topic that is of interest to your customers, it will increase your influence in the marketplace. It may also make sense to give away a sample of your product. The key is to ensure that you can provide the service economically, and that you present it well. A free offer should benefit you in the following ways:

- **the free material given away establishes the quality of your product in the marketplace**
- **it attracts potential customers for your paid-for products**
- **it attracts links from other websites, which in turn drives up your ranking on search engines**

The most extensive use of free giveaways by small companies is in the software industry. Nearly all consumer-oriented software programs are now available as time-limited free trials. Customers thereby get the opportunity to try out the product before they have to actually commit to purchasing it. As there is almost no cost involved in distributing this trial software, the risk for the software seller is very low.

If you sell a physical product or a service, having a free offer might be a big burden for your business. But if you can find a way to put the free product into the hands of your target audience, then this is definitely a strategy worth pursuing.

Flag up your Web address everywhere

Put your Web address on everything you send out, including your packaging, products and literature. It serves as a reminder to your customers of where they can go to get service and also provides a reference for potential new customers who may come across your product.

Promote your Web address in other media

Promote your Web address in traditional media. If you use print or radio advertising, see if you can incorporate your website and your Web address into future advertising. If you are able to get on TV or radio to talk about your product, you might be able to refer to your website as a resource to get more information. (It is a big help if you have an easy-to-remember domain name.)

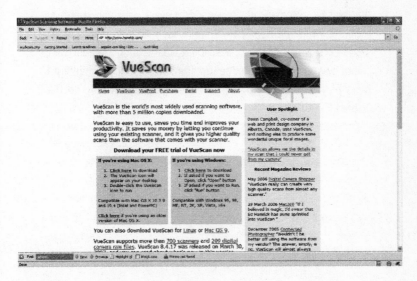

VueScan is a software product developed by a very small company in the US and marketed through the Web with a free trial download.

Give your customers a reason to return to the site

Think about the reasons that might entice you to regularly return to a supplier's site. If your site contains good reference information, or some information of interest that is regularly updated, there is a much better chance that you will visit the site again or refer someone else to the site.

Use e-mail to retain and develop existing customers

Your business probably sends out hundreds of e-mails every day, and these can form part of your strategy to promote your products or services to new and existing customers. The simplest way is to set up a standard e-mail signature on your company's e-mail system that will be automatically appended to every e-mail you send. It should contain your company's name, web address, and a short section (10 words or fewer) describing what is unique about your company. You can also vary the signature occasionally, to highlight areas of your business that your existing customers may not be aware of.

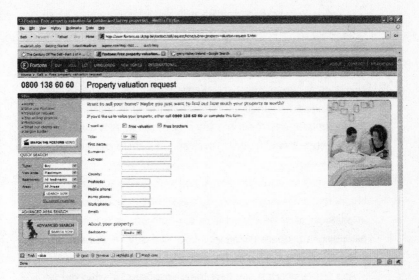

Foxtons, like most estate agents, offer a free property valuation for prospective sellers and feature this service prominently on their site. Free initial consultations are a way to obtain sales leads for any service company.

E-mail newsletters

Sending relevant offers to your existing customers who have agreed to receive e-mails from you is a useful way of keeping in touch and assuring them that you value their business.

It's also a good idea to send an e-mail newsletter to existing customers. But make sure you ask for customers' consent before you add them to any mailing list. In addition, give customers the opportunity to sign up for your newsletter via your website. If you are on a tight budget, you can use a free service such as Yahoo Groups (**www.yahoogroups.com**) to manage your list, or you can use a paid service to publish your newsletter without external advertising. Your hosting company may also offer this service for an extra charge.

Discussion boards and blogs

The Internet is primarily a social environment, where friends and acquaintances exchange information and keep in touch. Finding an appropriate way to fit into the social environment could be a cost-effective way of getting your name out there and attracting new business.

The first step is to get acquainted with blogs and discussion boards that are relevant to your business. You can learn a lot just by listening to what people have to say both on discussion boards belonging to other people in your industry, including your competitors, or on websites that relate to your local area.

As a businessperson, you have to be circumspect in what you say on a discussion board or on the comments section of a blog. Never be unfriendly or rude, even if the other person appears to be unreasonable. There is also no point in denigrating a competitor's products. It is very important always to disclose that you are in the business and to say whom you are working for.

It is important to understand the rules of the forum, even if you do not always agree with them. The forum is not a public resource; it is ultimately the property of some manager and administrator, and they are entitled to run it as they see fit.

Writing a blog

The idea of having a blog as part of your website was described in Chapter 2. If you believe that you can produce sufficient content of interest, having a blog can be a way of giving your business a human face and keeping your customers informed about all aspects of your company.

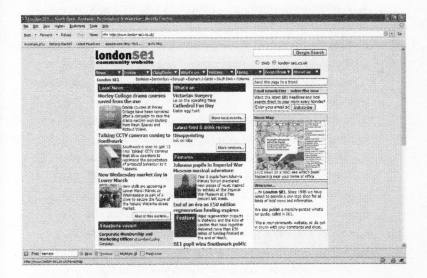

Many communities have local sites which display information about the area. Pay careful attention to these sites and see if they offer an opportunity to reach a new audience. They often include discussion boards and other features.

Viral marketing

An innovative way to get your message out is by using viral marketing. The power of viral marketing is that the message spreads rapidly through e-mail and word of mouth. Rather than the message being delivered directly to the audience by an advertisement, it is passed on by people who have received it already and are impressed enough to forward it to friends. The Internet marketing expert Ralph Wilson describes the six simple principles of viral marketing as follows:

1. **it gives away products or services (for example, it supplies entertainment, or provides a free service, such as the Hotmail e-mail service)**
2. **it provides for effortless transfer to others (i.e., the message can be forwarded on easily through e-mail or by word-of-mouth)**
3. **it scales easily from small to very large (because it is very hard to predict whether a particular viral marketing effort will take hold and grow explosively)**
4. **it exploits common motivations and behaviours (the effort has to have a reasonably widespread appeal)**
5. **it utilises existing communication networks (i.e., it can be sent by e-mail or linked to sites on the Web)**
6. **it takes advantage of others' resources (recipients of the message are the people who will actually distribute it)**

(See **www.wilsonweb.com/ wmt5/ viral-principles.htm**)
Although most of us have heard of and seen viral marketing, it is very difficult to implement effectively. So think about how these techniques might work for you on a small scale at first.

The most likely ideas to work for a small company might be:

- **a video demonstration of your product, where something interesting or dramatic happens**
- **a regular e-mail mailing list which is always informative and topical**
- **a time-limited, free giveaway of a relevant low-priced product or piece of software**

Paid-for for advertising

If you need to build your audience quickly and if your margins are big enough to sustain it, don't shy away from paid advertising on the Internet.

The first step to advertising online is to look at the economics. You need to understand how much you can afford to spend on acquiring a new customer. Here is one approach to doing this.

Calculate your average net margin for your business. You can do this quite easily by comparing your profit with your turnover. If your turnover is £100,000 and your profit is £20,000, then your net margin is 20 percent.

Then calculate the average net profit per customer. To do this, divide the profit of your business by the number of customers you provided a service to over the last year. Let's say that you had 400 customers:

$$\frac{£20,000/\text{year}}{400 \text{ customers}} = £50 \text{ profit per customer}$$

That means your average profit per customer last year was £50. If you were going to spend money to get new customers, and you wanted to see a payback on your investment within a year or so, you would have to make sure you did not spend more than £50 on obtaining each customer.

This figure should be in the back of your mind when planning your ad spend, so that you can be assured of a good payback on your investment.

Pay-per-click advertising and Google Adwords

You can advertise with Google Adwords for as little as a few pounds a day. Your text or graphical ads are then presented alongside Google search results. You only pay when someone actually clicks on your ad to get to your site. The price per click will depend on how popular the particular keyword is. Prices start as low as a few pence per click, and go up to £30 or £40 per click in certain specialised areas where there is extremely high demand (such as semi-conductors and medical litigation).

The big benefit of Google Adwords for the small advertiser is that you only have to pay when it actually works and a visitor is drawn to your site. Also, because you can set a budget, you can carefully control your daily spend.

Bear in mind how much it costs to bring a visitor to your site and convert him or her into a paying customer. You can use this with the profit-per-customer figure we calculated earlier to estimate what proportion of visitors to the site you will need to convert into

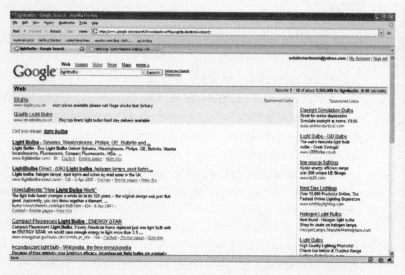

Google ads are shown above and to the right of the main results when you search on Google, and are clearly marked as 'Sponsored Links'.

customers in order to justify the cost of the advertising. Let's say that the cost per click is 40 pence. The required conversion rate can be calculated as follows:

$$\frac{\text{cost per click}}{\text{profit per customer}} = \frac{£0.40}{£50} = 0.008 = 0.8 \text{ percent}$$

This means that you would need to convert just under 1% of visitors to your site into paying customers in order to make your advertising viable. You will need to monitor the performance of your website to ensure that you are obtaining satisfactory

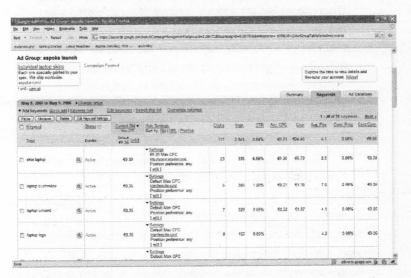

Managing the keywords for a Google Adwords campaign. At the top of the page is the ad that is part of the campaign. On the left-hand side is the list of keywords that trigger the ad. The 'Current Bid' is the maximum amount that may be paid for click-throughs on that keyword. The CTR (click-through ratio) is the proportion of people who clicked on the ad when they saw it.

conversions. Use the Google Analytics website tracking tool (see later in this chapter) or a similar tool to help you monitor how successful your site is in converting customers.

There are two main ways you can improve your conversion rate.

1. **Fine-tune your keywords to ensure that you only target people who are likely to have a general interest in buying your products or services. For example, you might get a better conversion rate for an advertisement on the keywords 'plumber battersea' than you would for a more general advertisement on the keywords 'plumber london'.**
2. **Improve your website 'experience' so that it is easier for potential customers to move from being passive visitors checking your website into active enquirers who leave a query or make a purchase. For example, you could have a landing page that brings click-through visitors directly to the relevant information they are looking for, rather than dropping them at the home page or on a product page.**

Other pay-per-click advertising

There are a number of other pay-per-click advertising operators apart from Google, in particular Yahoo! At the time of writing, Google continues to be the best-designed and easiest system to use, although there may be better value to be obtained from other providers.

Facebook is also emerging as a provider of pay-per-click advertising. Facebook has many special features which Google AdWords cannot offer, for example, that it can target your existing customers (people who have 'liked' your page), their friends, people in a specific demographic (for example women, 18–25), people living within a certain distance of a specific town or city, and so on.

There is one big difference between Facebook and Google or Yahoo in terms of advertising however. Google searchers are almost always looking for something when they visit Google, and they are likely to be close to the point of purchasing a product or service, and they are likely to be in an inquisitive mode. Facebook users, by contrast, do not usually have a specific agenda. The jury is still out on what this means for advertisers. However, it seems likely that Facebook advertising is best suited to longer-term awareness campaigns and to lifestyle services. Google on the other hand is a bit better suited to the types of products customers seek out, like products and services for business, or household products to meet a specific need.

Banner advertising

Many larger websites offer banner advertising, which is paid for on a 'cost per impression' basis. This means that you pay for every time the ad is shown, whether anybody clicks on it or not. Ads are typically priced by the 'cost per thousand' impressions (CPM for short).

There are a number of big disadvantages to banner advertising for small businesses:

- you will typically be expected to commit to 10,000 or more impressions, which will cost you at least a few hundred pounds
- once the campaign is underway, it is generally very hard to make adjustments to it
- because you are a small purchaser, you may find yourself paying a higher rate for the same ad spots than your larger competitors

- you will probably need to invest in good-quality graphic designers in order to come up with a compelling banner that will entice the people who see it to click on it
- conversion rates will be lower than for search advertising, because customers are not specifically looking for a product when they click on the ad

As before, try to fit the cost of the banner ad into your sales model. How many visits to your website is the ad campaign likely to generate based on your or typical industry experience? For example, if a banner ad campaign has a CPM of £20, and the click-through rate is 1 percent, then the cost per visitor will be 20p (1 percent of £20). If 2 percent of these visitors (that is, one in 50) are converted into customers, the cost per conversion will be £10 (20p × 50).

However, if the price is right, and the website on which you are advertising is strongly linked to what you are selling, banner advertising may be a good option for you.

Unconventional approaches

Many advertising opportunities are too small to appear on the radar for major firms, but may be relevant to you as a small company with a niche audience. For example, there may be an e-mail newsletter which is read by your target market, and which offers opportunities for advertising. Many of these are run by small publishers, who can offer attractive rates. If the quality of the content is good and there is a reasonable readership, it could turn out to be a useful deal.

For this type of advertising, again, think about the financial equation, in other words, whether the advertising is likely to result in valuable conversions.

However, it is not as easy to track performance as when using a conventional approach, and the levels of response will be much lower, because the people who see the ad are not specifically looking for your product. Also, the benefit you get from the ad may be indirect as well as direct. For example, it may promote awareness of your company in the industry, and may generate goodwill. While this will not produce an immediate return, it may have value in the longer term.

Affiliate marketing

If you are selling a product online, you may be able to benefit from affiliate marketing. On the Internet, this means having another website (the affiliate) link to your website, and agreeing to give the owner of that website a proportion of the revenues that result from people clicking on the link and visiting your site.

The advantage of this system is that you share the risk with the affiliate; if nothing is sold, they do not get paid. However, it does involve some fixed costs:

- **you must have a technical solution to track affiliate click-through**
- **you must promote your affiliate offer to the right kind of websites and convince them to sign up**

Both of these will require a significant investment of time and money, or the help of a specialist in the area.

Is affiliate marketing right for you?

Affiliate marketing doesn't suit every online business, but if you meet at least eight of the following criteria, it may work for you, according to professional affiliate manager Durk Price (see

**www.site-reference.com/ articles/ Website-Development/
The-10-Most-Important-Criteria-You-Must- Meet-to-Attract-
Top-Affiliates.html**):

- you are able to sell the product nationally and internationally
- your product is fairly unique
- you have a fairly strong brand name
- you have large enough margins to be able to make an aggressive payout to your affiliates
- you know how much you want to spend to get customers
- your pricing is competitive
- the price per sale is big enough to justify the affiliate marketer's efforts (usually at least £40)
- you have a good conversion rate for visitors to your site
- you have a good e-commerce system that doesn't put off users
- your website is attractive and compelling

Affiliate marketing isn't for everyone, but if your product fits into the categories above, then you should certainly consider it.

Coupon marketing

Coupon marketing entails offering your product at a heavily discounted rate (usually 40–60 percent) through a promoter like Livingsocial or Citydeals (known as Groupon outside Europe). The promoter markets the discount offer to its massive database of e-mail subscribers. The customers sign up for the offer by paying in advance, and the promoter holds on to 30–50 per cent of the payment to cover its own costs and profit margin.

This approach can be highly effective at attracting new customers. It is attractive for advertisers because there is no up-front expenditure on marketing. However, the large discount that the promoter will require leaves the advertiser with no profit, and possibly a loss from the transaction. There have been stories about advertisers finding that they are overwhelmed, and not in a position to fulfil the coupon the customer has purchased. Another frequent problem is that very few of these customers turn into long-term customers.

Like any promotion strategy, it has to be financially evaluated. You need to do your calculations, in conjunction with an accountant if necessary, to find out if promoting through these offers will work for you. If you do go through with one of these offers, you need to have a concerted plan for converting these one-off customers into repeat, long-term customers. At a minimum you need to collect their e-mail address and you will also have to entice them with attentive customer service and with further offers.

Auction sites

It is a good idea to get on a major auction site, most likely eBay. eBay has become an international reference site for people looking for well-priced goods from reputable sellers. Any business, no matter how small, can list on ebay.com for a small fee, and use it as a channel to offer discounted products. The cost of the discount, and the cost of the listing may affect profit in the short term, but if your product is popular, it will get customers familiar with your product and lead to longer-term sales.

Putting up an item for sale on eBay seems quite daunting at first. There is some setup involved and you have to sell by auction, which is something few businesses are used to. However, if you have done your research and you take care to provide good customer service, it's quite easy.

The first thing to do is to research similar products being sold on eBay at present. This will give you important information:

- **who your competitors are, and where they are from**
- **what the typical prices are**
- **whether many sales are being made (you can find out how many auctions are in progress, and whether they are being successfully concluded as sales)**

The next step is to jump in and offer something for sale. Although eBay has a feature to allow sales at a fixed price, this is not open to first-time eBayers, so you will have to put your items up for auction. You can set a 'reserve' price, however, which will mean that you don't have to sell the product unless you get a reasonable bid for it.

To sell, you have to register, and you will need to give credit-card details. eBay does this to ensure that as a seller you can be traced, and as a means to collect your fees.

A good description

The description you provide of your product is critical. The most important thing to consider is the title. This is the first thing customers will see, and it is also used when customers are searching for products. Your title should be highly descriptive – it should include information such as the manufacturer, the product name, the model number, the colour and anything else that customers are likely to search for. Don't bother using words that customers are unlikely to use to search, such as 'beautiful' or 'excellent'. These may be good words for your main description, but they should not form part of your title.

The description should explain the features of the product and clearly state whether it is new, refurbished or used. If it is used, then the condition of the product needs to be stated frankly.

Clear photographs

The photograph you provide will make a big difference to your ability to sell. You don't need to be a professional photographer, but you should take care to take the best photograph you can.

- Use a fully automated digital camera. You don't need a high-spec camera, just a simple one that's easy to use. A digital camera will allow you to take reasonably good quality pictures quickly, check the results and upload them on to your computer. It's not essential that it has a high resolution – photographs used on the Internet are rarely larger than 2 megapixels anyway.

- Use a tripod if you have one or can borrow one. It makes it easier to take a photo that isn't blurred. It also leaves your hands free while you are getting ready to take your photo.

- Use the best lighting you can. The easiest way is to use natural daylight. If the light is too intense, however, it will create unattractive shadows. You can reduce the shadows by using a reflector, by diffusing the light by closing the blinds, or simply by moving to a room that faces north. If you take photos of objects regularly it might be worth looking for a photo tent and a flash system to produce more consistent results.

- Avoid using the built-in flash on your camera. It usually produces a very flat photograph when used at close range.

- Find a good backdrop and avoid clutter. The best photographs are taken against a plain background, with few or no extraneous objects.

- Fill the frame. You need to get close enough so that your object takes up most of the photograph.

- Provide something in the picture to give an impression of scale. It could be your hand holding the object, or a ruler, or some other item that will give your customers an idea of size.

- Use a photo-editing package to enhance your photo and make it the right size for displaying on the screen. Many packages allow you to adjust colour and contrast. You can also crop your photos if there is a lot of empty space around the item you are selling. Your computer or your digital camera may have come with a suitable photo-editing package. Alternatively, you can download a free package such as Google Picasa (**http://picasa.google.com**), which provides easy-to-use editing facilities, or the Gimp (**www.gimp.org/windows**), which is harder to use but is more sophisticated. If you do a lot of photographic work and can justify the expense, consider buying a package such as Corel Paintshop Pro or Adobe Photoshop.

One problem you may face when you first list on eBay is that as a new seller, you have no 'feedback' on your profile. Your feedback is how prospective customers evaluate your reliability as an eBay seller. Regular eBay sellers even get special recognition and markings on their profiles.

The only real solution to this problem is to get into the market and make some sales. However, one way to build up some initial credibility is to make some purchases on eBay and make sure that they are successfully concluded. The seller will leave feedback about your performance as a buyer, and you will also get the opportunity to leave feedback about the seller. When you do this, be sure to use the same eBay username as you plan to use to make your sales.

You can also improve buyers' perceptions by giving a full description of your business and a link to your website as part of the description. Prospective buyers will be happier dealing with you if they can find out some information about your company.

Measuring your success

One area that is often an afterthought in web development is measuring the success of a site. After you have invested time and money in your site, you will want to get some feedback about your website's performance. At the most basic level you will want to know how many people are visiting your site, where they are coming from, and what they are looking at. Next, you may want to analyse how your customers interact with the site – how they typically behave when they get there. You may also want to do a detailed analysis of the most valuable sources of links to your site.

There are many good tools on the market for measuring your website, so many, in fact, that you may find it confusing to select a statistics package. Some are available for free, and others you have to pay for. There are technical implications in implementing statistics packages, since they may require you to have software installed on your Web server or on your office computer. Your hosting provider may set up a statistics package for you based on one of the free packages.

Any package will give you the basic information about your website. The principal statistics it will give you are:

- **number of 'hits'**
- **number of page accesses**
- **number of visitors**

- basic information about the users (for example, what country they are visiting from)
- most commonly visited pages on your site

This information should be a great help for you in evaluating the success of your site. However, there are a couple of provisos to consider when you look at the statistics:

- some of the statistics are dramatic, rather than factual. While it may sound exciting when your competitor tells you that their site gets 2 million hits per month, it tells you very little about how the site is actually performing. Many of the hits are likely to be downloads of images on pages, rather than actual page views. The number of page accesses or number of visitors is a better measure of the traffic a site is receiving.
- not all statistics packages measure page accesses, visits and visitors the same way, so it may not be possible to make direct comparisons between different sites.
- don't take information such as the countries that visitors are from too literally. For a number of reasons, this information may be incorrect or misleading. For example, .com addresses are assumed by some software packages to be in the US, but this is not necessarily the case.

While any package will give you the basic information, you will need a more sophisticated package if you want to better understand your marketplace. One system you should definitely consider is

Google Analytics. It provides quite sophisticated features, and is offered free of charge by Google.

Even if you decide not to use Google Analytics, the features of this package are similar to many others. So take time to understand what this type of tool can do.

Why does Google offer Google Analytics for free?

Google acquired Google Analytics (which was originally developed by a company called Urchin) in order to provide enhanced services to its advertising customers and to make its advertising offerings even more attractive. It has integrated Google Analytics with its Adwords advertising product. The benefits for business users are manifold:

- Google Analytics can help advertisers determine which advertising is the most effective, in terms of converting into purchases or enquiries
- the statistical information is likely to attract decision-makers to visit the Adwords site on a daily or weekly basis, prompting them to consider using Adwords to promote their businesses
- Google Analytics becomes a key part of business users' website operations, making them more likely to stick with Google

There is also another benefit for Google in giving Google Analytics away for free – it gives Google a unique insight into consumer behaviour and website preferences. Although your browsing behaviour or the stats from your website don't mean much in isolation, the information can be put together with stats from other sites and other consumers to form a much bigger picture. Google could potentially combine the information it collects from Google Analytics with information from its search engine to build detailed profiles of individual businesses' traffic patterns as well as the Web-browsing habits of hundreds of millions of individual consumers.

There are immediate benefits for businesses but, in the longer term, businesses and consumers are going to have to decide whether it is really wise to give Google such unfettered access to their internal business information and details about customers. Equally, Google will have to make sure that it has policies in place to ensure that privacy of businesses and consumers is sufficiently respected.

Google Analytics features

Google Analytics is implemented by putting some code into every page on your site which ensures that every access to your website is relayed to the Google server. This raw data is then collated into regular reports which you can access through the Google Adwords website.

The information is presented as a wide range of graphs and maps. At its most basic level, Google Analytics tells you how many visits you have, how many are first-time visitors, what countries or regions your visitors are coming from, and what search engine or other website they used to find your site. You can also delve into much more detail, and there are special reports oriented around the needs of the site manager and the person responsible for Web marketing.

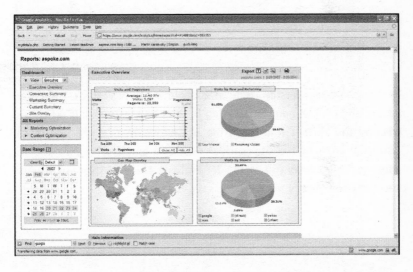

Google Analytics – basic information. The charts tell you how many visitors you've had, whether they are first-time visitors and what website they come from. The map shows what areas of the world they are visiting from. You can use the calendar to narrow down the statistics to cover only one particular time period.

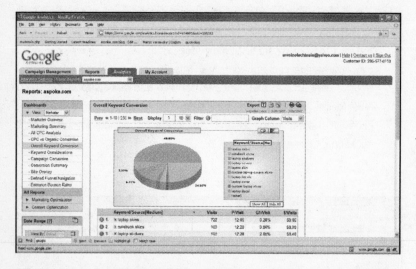

The keyword conversion tool in Google Analytics tracks whether advertising click-through is resulting in sales and enquiries. It measures whether the visitors who reach the site by means of these ads reach particular goals on the site (such as making a purchase or e-mailing an enquiry). This allows you to rapidly evaluate the effectiveness of your keywords and modify them if necessary.

Google Analytics allows you to figure out which parts of your site are the most popular, and which links customers are clicking on. This gives you some clues about customers' behaviour.

These are just a small selection of the reports that Google Analytics offers. There are a host of features oriented at marketing needs, website optimisation and overall executive website management. It is a good idea to learn about all the features and decide which ones might be of use to your business.

Applying the information and reviewing your strategy

Before you get carried away with the many different statistical programs and techniques available, remember that the most important part of any measurement system is *you*, the manager who interprets the information and acts upon it.

Once you have the information from the site, you have to invest the time to understand it and to act upon it appropriately. If customers are coming to your website but not finding their way into the most important sections, then what is wrong? It may be that the links to the deeper pages are not obvious, or that the page is taking too long to load. You need to take remedial action, fast.

As you make changes to your website, you can gauge what customers find important, and whether something about the site is putting them off making enquiries or making purchases. For example, you might put prices up on your site for a week and then remove them again. You can monitor the traffic and see if the price information attracts customers, or motivates them to look around the site more.

Don't be too disappointed if your first efforts at Web marketing don't pay off as well as you had hoped for. If you've followed the suggestions in this chapter and your initial investment wasn't too large, you will be able to try again, with a slightly different approach. It takes time to learn how best to apply the tools and to find out what will work well for your business. On the bright side, it is very easy to change your online marketing to reflect any feedback you receive and the information you get from your statistics tools.

4 BUILDING THE 'BACK END' OF YOUR INTERNET BUSINESS

You've thought about what you're going to sell on the Internet and how you're going to market it. You have a plan for your website. But how will you build the 'back end', the bit that will link the website into your production and other systems?

It may be that you don't need any special Web-based systems at the outset, or that your needs are very straightforward. But sooner or later, if your online business becomes established and grows, you will want to develop something more sophisticated.

The back-end systems you require will depend on what your business and your approach will be. You may need shopping cart software to have a good, smooth purchasing process on your website. An order management system may be required to ensure that every order is tracked through to completion. You may need a system to track customer service e-mails and phone calls. If you are in a service industry, you may want to think about a booking system of some sort. Although the requirements are always quite different, the basic issues and concerns should be the same.

Any business developing a website project with a significant technical element will have the following concerns:

- **Will there be a good return on the investment?**
- **Will this cost be more than planned?**
- **Will it be delivered soon enough?**
- **Will this take too much of my energy and effort?**

These concerns strain the minds of the boards of the biggest companies in the world, even though they have access to the best expertise and have plenty of cash to deal with problems that arise. Overruns are very frequent and many projects end up cancelled or as failures. Return on investment is often not as good as anticipated.

As a small business, you have a further disadvantage. You and your staff probably aren't that experienced at running IT projects. You can't afford to hire a large team of consultants to set up your e-commerce platform. You aren't sitting on a cash mountain and you can't go to the markets and ask for more if you run out. If the project absorbs too much of your time, it will seriously affect your current business, and if the project goes seriously wrong, you might even find yourself out of business.

Managing your back-end development

Before you get into the nitty-gritty of planning and developing your project, it's wise to make sure that your project has a clear management structure.

At a bare minimum, you need to put in place some of the following roles for any IT development project which you think is likely to take more than a few weeks or cost more than a few thousand pounds.

- **Project Sponsor.** This is the person at senior management level who is driving the project and takes ultimate responsibility for it. In a small business, this will typically be the owner and manager of the business, but it need not be.
- **Steering Group.** The steering group should bring together the main areas of interest for the project. For example, an order management system might have a representative from customer services, operations and finance. The marketing department might also nominate someone to represent the interests of the customer in the development. The steering group should meet every few weeks to consider project progress.

One key role of a steering group is to review the project at a high level, and decide whether it should be continued to the next stage. One mistake commonly made by steering committees in companies of all sizes is failing to stop a project when it becomes clear that is not likely to meet its stated objectives. If a project looks like it's not going to deliver the benefits your company needs, be prepared to end it before the costs get out of hand.

Your project may be too small to justify the expense of a steering group, but you certainly need to consider how you will ensure that all the people who will use the system are represented in its development and to make sure you have a clear mechanism for controlling the project.

- **Project Manager.** The project manager is in control of the project and makes decisions on a day-to-day basis. He or she may also have some other role in the project, for example writing use cases or specifications, and need not be working full-time on the project.

At the outset, make a 'best guess' estimate of how long the project will take to complete. If your company is not experienced in developing IT systems, it's best to find a way to keep the project quite short, no longer than two or three months. Don't be afraid to simplify and split up the project if necessary.

Develop a business case

Every software project, no matter how small, needs to have a business case which the project sponsor and the steering group agree with and are prepared to buy into. That means there has to be a clear understanding of the benefits that the project will bring to the business. If possible, these benefits should be quantified.

A business case might include the following:

- **a problem statement, outlining the particular problem or opportunity**
- **a description, in the broadest terms, of the type of solution envisaged**
- **an estimate of the time and effort that will be involved in implementing the new system**
- **an estimate of the benefits that will accrue from the new system**

Where possible, the costs and benefits to your company should be worked out in pounds and pence. Even a rough estimate will allow you to manage your budget, and to measure the success of the business later on.

Your business case only needs to be a page or two long at the outset. It may become more detailed and complex as necessary in due course. You can refer to the business case as the project proceeds to ensure everything remains within the original plan.

Consider how you are going to get a return on your investment. For IT projects in small companies, the most appropriate measure is probably to calculate the 'payback period'. Put simply, this is the amount of time you estimate it will take for the investment you make to pay for itself. If you have estimated the cost of the system, and the benefits that the system will bring, it will be easy to calculate the payback period.

The payback period that is acceptable to you will depend on your industry. If your industry is fast moving and there are constant changes and developments, then a payback period of a few years may be acceptable. If your industry is always changing, and there is a risk that the system you install may become obsolete, then aim to have a payback period of two years or less.

There are many technical methods for calculating return on investment for a project, such as the 'internal rate of return' (which indicates whether an investment is worth pursuing) or 'net present value' (which shows the projected profitability of an investment), and you may want your accountant to look into these for you if you are considering a large, long-term project.

How you go about building or acquiring your back-end systems will depend on your situation and your business strategy. You may find that many others in your industry are already implementing a particular software package or hosted solution for their businesses, and it will probably make sense to follow in their footsteps as quickly as possible so that you can keep up with them. You will also benefit from the experience the IT vendors have built up in your sector, and as a result the implementation should be faster, the risks will be lower, and the costs will be easier to control.

On the other hand, if you want to break new ground with your system, doing something that has not been done before and that will constitute a big differentiator between you and your competitors, you may have to develop one from scratch or tailor one to meet your needs. This approach is riskier: it's harder to have a real fix on what the costs might be, and the project will probably take longer and absorb more of your time. There is more information about the different ways of implementing your back end later in this chapter. If your back-end plans have a major strategic goal such as this, that goal should also form part of your company's vision statement.

Develop a vision statement

You have already developed a business case that addresses the generalities of the project. At this stage, it's helpful to develop a more focused 'vision statement'. The vision statement should form a short summary of the rationale for the system and what the needs are. It should address both the general issues (for example, the need to have a smoother ordering process and better customer service) and the specifics (that users need to be able to order online and then check the status of their order through a Web page).

Make absolutely sure that everyone involved agrees this vision statement. It will form a solid basis for development later on, and you will need to be able to refer to it at a later stage as the project progresses. It will make it easier to determine what should be included in the project and what should be left out as the project develops.

At the outset, a vision statement will only contain two or three sentences. It can be developed into a more detailed statement later on if needed. An example of a vision statement might be:

In order to grow, the company needs to be able to deal with orders for our product more rapidly and accurately. The new order management system will deal with orders from the Internet and ensure that they are processed quickly and can be tracked precisely. The system will benefit customers by making the ordering process easier and improving delivery times, and benefit staff by reducing the amount of time spent dealing with queries and paperwork.

Note that at this stage, no mention is made of the types of system that will be considered or the technical details of any solution.

Write a requirements document

The 'requirements document' is basically a detailed list of the things that the system should do. It needs to contain as much information and be as specific as possible. At the same time, it should avoid stating exactly how the system is to be implemented – that should be determined during the development.

There are many ways to approach the development of a requirements document. One of the most effective is to begin by understanding the needs of the people who will be the users of the system. A good starting point is to list all the 'actors' who will be involved with the system. Actors are the people who access the system or otherwise depend on it. The list can also include other systems that may be accessed by it. In a typical online system, the actors could be:

- **site visitors**
- **registered customers**
- **sales staff**

- customer service staff
- order management system
- system administrator

For each of these groups, list the 'use cases' for them. These are the ways in which these actors will interact with the system. In many situations, the same 'use cases' will apply to a number of different groups of actors.

For a website ordering system, the use cases could be:

- browse catalogue
- make an order
- pay for an order
- view customer's outstanding orders
- modify an order
- cancel an order

At this stage, the various lists you have generated will begin to give you an idea of the complexity of the system. Remember, each use case will contain multiple screens and involve a number of pieces of data, and the system will have to tie all of these elements together.

For each use case, you need to detail the steps an actor would go through to complete the use case.

Example use case

Actor: Customer
Use case: Make an order

After browsing the online catalogue, the customer chooses a product of interest and clicks 'add to shopping cart'. If there is any special information required (such as a size or colour), that should be also entered at this stage. The customer will then be given the opportunity to add appropriate accessories for the product to their order (for example, if they order a light fitting, they may be asked if they wish to buy a bulb to go with it). The customer can then return to browsing and add products to the order, or he or she may want to go straight to the payment process.

What not to do

At this stage, it's best to focus on the systems and the functional requirements and not to spend too much time worrying about the technical implementation. For example, any decision on the operating system to be used, or the type of database that will be required, should be postponed, although if there are any special requirements, they should certainly be noted.

How detailed should the specification be?

At the beginning, avoid producing overly complicated specifications. Provide details for two or three types of user, and go into some detail on up to two or three use cases for each type of user. Your specification need not be longer than three or four pages, and it may be much shorter if you are simply planning to implement an existing industry solution.

However, you may need to produce more detailed specifications as the project goes on. If you decide to develop your own software, or to customise existing software, the developer will want to agree how the software should work in much more detail.

Decide your approach and produce a plan

You now have the basic materials to begin to plan for the development of your system. At this stage you definitely need to get technical resources involved, and you will have to make a decision on the development approach you will take.

Approaches to development

In practice, the development approach is the critical phase of the project where many of the key decisions will be taken. It's important to get this stage of the project as correct as possible and to obtain agreement among stakeholders. You may also benefit from getting the opinions of outside experts and consultants at this point.

Develop manual or semi-manual processes

All that said, it is sometimes possible to develop a simple but trustworthy system based on paper or in an Excel (or similar) spreadsheet, rather than splashing out on new equipment. Many businesses overlook this possibility, but if your requirements are simple, or if you are not really yet sure what your requirements are, this could turn out to be a really good short-term approach. You will still need to go through the steps of analysing your requirements and then putting in place a paper system that will meet your needs.

The main disadvantage of a paper system is that it requires a lot of manual work, which takes up employees' time. It may not be able to grow quickly enough with your business. It requires a lot of training to make sure nothing gets lost, and if all of your operations are not on a single site, it may be difficult to keep track of the pieces of paper and computer files.

Hosting, the Cloud and outsourced solutions

The services that are available on a per-use basis on the Internet are sometimes now referred to as 'The Cloud'. The idea of calling it the cloud is as follows. These are services that are at some remove from us. We are not overly concerned with how exactly they work and they may be somewhat opaque (in that sense, they are fuzzy, like a real cloud). They are present and part of the environment and not something that we specifically have to build.

Of course the cloud metaphor is only partly true. Cloud services are hosted on real servers, and there is still a real cost to operating them. Like any other computer system, they are subject to technical hitches. To use the Cloud effectively, you are dependent on a reliable high-quality broadband connection.

However, there is real merit in these services. The idea of the Cloud is to take a lot of the work of IT away from the business and hand it over to a specialised outside company.

'The Cloud' is part of the broader business strategy of IT outsourcing.

Rather than having your own in-house software systems, you can use the 'hosted solutions' available through the Internet. For example, the Paypal payment system described in Chapter 2 is an example of a hosted solution commonly used by small businesses. eBay is another. Rather than developing your own payment systems or auction systems on your website, you simply tap into theirs. This makes e-commerce viable, even on a small scale.

The use of hosted services (sometimes called Application Service Providers or ASPs) is an example of IT outsourcing.

IT outsourcing has become a buzzword in business circles. Many large companies have decided that managing websites, e-mail, computers and the multitude of IT systems that are required for a modern business are not core activities, and that it would be better to get another, more specialised company to take over this area of the business. What happens in practice is that the IT division of the large company is separated from the rest of the business and is sold to an IT firm (e.g., Accenture, HP or Cap Gemini) that has the breadth and capability to manage the business. As part of the sale, the IT specialist will agree to provide services to the company for a certain price. The whole deal is subject to a complex outsourcing contract which covers a multitude of issues, such as the types of service to be provided, commitments on quality, a transition plan and an operating plan. These deals often run into hundreds of millions of pounds and can take years to put into action.

For a small business, the context of outsourcing is quite different, but many of the concerns and issues are the same, albeit on a much smaller scale. Outsourcing might entail using IT systems that you access over the Internet and which belong to another company, in order to meet your IT needs. Rather than charging a large up-front price for equipment and software licences, you pay a usage fee every month, or every time you use the system.

The hosted application may be a key system that you use every day (e.g., your customer database) or it may be an application you use relatively infrequently (such as a recruitment system).

There are now many companies on the market which provide hosted solutions that are suitable for small and medium-sized businesses. Consider whether one of these systems might be suitable for your needs. The solutions offered fall into two main categories:

1. Sector-specific solutions

A number of sectors have their own hosted platforms for sharing information and managing their businesses. For example, almost all travel agents worldwide use a Customer Reservation Systems to manage their information. These systems not only provide the ability to reserve a seat or a room; they also manage all of the travel agent's other business information, including notes on passengers' individual preferences, bills for clients, daily, weekly and monthly management activity and profitability reports, and so on. The systems can also provide web-based solutions for customers of the travel agent for added convenience. Some of the operators of these systems include the major global booking engines such as Sabre, Galileo and Amadeus, but smaller companies offering more specialised solutions have also entered the fray.

Similarly, car dealers may join a network such as Auto Trader. The primary benefit of such a system is that it allows the customer to be part of a centralised system that makes it easy for end-customers to find the car they are looking for. However, it also provides a convenient way for dealers to manage information about their stock of vehicles. It may also allow them to access information about relevant vehicles that may be available for purchase in neighbouring areas.

2. General-purpose solutions

There are also many solutions available that can be applied to any number of different sectors. For example, in the area of Customer Relationship Management, which deals with the maintenance of lists of customers and sales leads, and ensures that leads are followed up and orders are dealt with, a number of solutions are available from international companies and these are designed specifically with the needs of small businesses in mind.

For example, **salesforce.com** provides a solution for small businesses for a yearly subscription of less than $1000. For that, you get access to an account, contact and activity management system similar to that used by large *Fortune 500* companies. However, as you grow your business, add more users, or need new features, your subscription fee will grow.

There are also smaller competitors, who can provide a less sophisticated product for a lower price. SugarCRM's 'Sugar on demand' product provides a similar service, at a slightly lower price level.

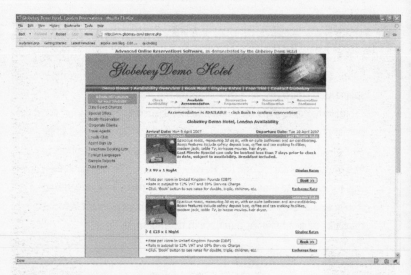

Similar solutions are available for many different sectors. Globekey, shown above, provides a system to manage room bookings for small and medium-sized hotels.

Google Docs (http://docs.google.com/) is envisaged as a web-based alternative to Microsoft Word, Excel and PowerPoint. You can prepare text documents, spreadsheets and presentations much as you could when using the Microsoft programs, although without some of the more advanced features. A big boon of Google Docs over using an ordinary office program is that you can easily and securely share documents, and earlier versions of documents will be automatically retained.

Benefits of a hosted solution in the Cloud

Ease of management. These hosted systems are extremely easy for a small business to manage. There is no need to buy or manage

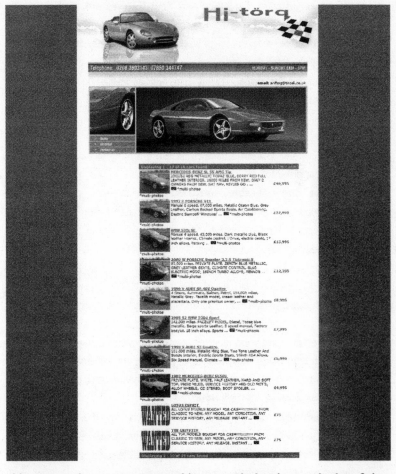

This motor sales company (www.hi-torq.co.uk) has invested a lot of time and effort in designing a website that fits in with their brand. However, the stock list is managed through autotrader.co.uk, and the stock list is shown as part of their website.

any server software. Upgrades and new features are generally implemented without your having to do or install anything.

Remote access. It is easy for workers to access the system when they are away from the office.

Always up to date. The system will generally be updated automatically with new features, without your having to buy licence upgrades.

Easier to finance. Regular, small payments rather than an up-front charge. You don't have to raise the money to pay for new software and hardware.

Unique and valuable features. Online systems, particular sector-specific systems, may offer features that are not available with any other type of system. For example, they offer access to sector-specific databases and purchasing facilities.

Disadvantages of a Cloud-based solution

Lack of customisation. You may not be able to customise the application as much as you need. Although the core of the application may suit your needs, there may be extras you would like to have put in place. You may be dependent on the outsourcing company to do this work, and they may not be willing to make any changes whatsoever to the system.

Dependency. You will be dependent on the hosting company and the quality of its infrastructure. Also, you will be depending on your Internet connection being completely reliable – if it is down for any reason, you won't have access to essential files.

Things to consider when choosing a Cloud-based solution

As well as considering the features of an outsourced solution, you should think about the following:

Dependability. You will be wholly dependent on the company providing the service, so you need to be confident that they have the technical, managerial and financial strength to support your business in the long term.

Speed. Can you access the application reasonably quickly over your Internet connection? If not, using the system will be frustrating for your staff.

Price. Don't just consider the up-front price. Many companies have cheap introductory offers for their basic start-up service. As you require new features or add new users, the prices may increase at a rapid rate. You should take your expansion plans into account as you evaluate the options.

Expansion. How will you expand the features of the system in the future, if necessary? Does the company plan to add the features you might need, or will they make it easy for you to implement them? Think carefully about whether you will really need these extra features.

Migration. If in the future you outgrow the system or have to stop using it for some reason, is there any way for you to export your data and move it to a new platform? It is critical that you have a way of accessing and managing your own data.

Buying a software package

Packaged software (also called 'off-the-shelf' software) is intended to be used by a large number of different users. The vast majority of software in use in the world is packaged software, including the operating system, word processing and e-mail software you use every day. You buy it and install it on your computer, and after some configuration, you are ready to go.

There are thousands of software packages on the market, and it's very likely that at least one of them will meet most of your needs.

The advantages of packaged software are enormous, if you can find the right package. This is especially the case for small businesses that may not be able to afford to develop a specialised system from scratch.

Advantages of packaged software

Generally speaking, prepackaged software is inexpensive and the quality is quite good. The reasons for this are as follows:

- **The product has been maturing for a number of years and the biggest weaknesses of the package have been sorted out over time.**
- **The cost of the product development has been divided among many customers and so the price is much lower.**
- **The larger cash flow available from a packaged software business means there are likely to be more development resources devoted to the development of the program, compared to programs that are developed in-house.**
- **There will be a lot of expertise available about the product if it is widely used. It is more likely that new employees will be familiar with the program already.**

Disadvantages of packaged software

- **The package may not suit you if you have very specialised needs.**
- **The package may not have the right features to give you the strategic advantage you need.**
- **The package may have the basic features you need, but it may require so much customisation and**

expansion in the future that the investment in the
package may not be worth the expense.

Packaged software in practice

All IT-aware businesses use packaged software to some extent.
In standard areas, where there are infrequent changes and where
you do not enjoy any strategic advantage over your competitors,
packaged software is probably your best option. Accounting
software is one area where packages predominate. Almost all
organisations have similar accounting practices, and therefore
require quite similar features from their basic accounting package.
Furthermore, there is little competitive advantage to be had from
having an accounting system that is different from everyone else's.

If you have specialised functions, however, the packaged solution
may not be suitable. You may have developed a special process which
requires special coordination and control. Although prepackaged
software might provide some support, it may not give you the specific
features you need to really make your process efficient and supply
the exact service you want. In this case you need to think about
customising the package or else writing a program from scratch.

However, just because you have unique processes and
requirements does not mean that you should dismiss using a
package. Many large companies have decided to standardise their
processes to meet the features of the complex and expensive
enterprise resource planning software such as SAP. These companies
have calculated that they gain little advantage from their unique
processes, and that it would be better to change the processes
rather than investing in rewriting the software to match up with the
current system. Consider whether your process is truly unique and
valuable, or just happens to be different from the industry standard
and could be easily adapted.

A note about open-source software

The idea of open-source software began with enthusiasts, researchers and networking specialists, but is now beginning to make a serious impact in the business sphere. In general terms, open-source software is not proprietary, meaning that the source of the software is available to all to modify and build upon as they see fit. The new software is then shared among the community to allow further development and improvement.

The most obvious benefit is that the software is free, although this is only one small factor to consider. The bigger advantage is that you are able to change the software as you see appropriate, and you can obtain support from a number of sources, not just the company you bought it from. You also benefit from the cushion of expertise that is available about the product.

If you are considering an open-source solution, assess the value it will deliver to your business. As with any software, don't just look at the initial expense; look at the overall cost over the lifetime of the system. Consider how you will get technical support; unless your company is big enough to have full-time administrators, you have to think about how you can get access to outside expertise when you need it (something you need to take into account whatever type of software you purchase).

Evaluating software

Evaluating packaged software can be a daunting process. The most important thing is to state your requirements, especially your core must-have features, and to check that the packages meet these needs. For example, if you are evaluating order management systems, you might produce a list like the following.

	Essential?	Package 1	Package 2
Enter an order	Yes	✓	✓
Edit an order	Yes		✓
Custom fields for order entry	No	✓	
Produce invoice	Yes	✓	✓
Produce standard reports	Yes		✓
Produce custom reports	No	✓	
Self-service facility for customers	No	✓	✓
Integrate with accounts package	Yes		✓

Don't just look at the features of the software. You also need to evaluate what are called 'non-functional' aspects of the software, as follows:

Usability. Is the software easy to work with? Can daily tasks be completed quickly without repetition?

Scalable. Is the system big enough to cope with your organisation's size and growth? The best way to evaluate this is to find out about other installations of the software of similar or larger size. Also, bear in mind that software designed for a much bigger organisation may require a more expensive platform and expensive support from consultants and maintenance staff.

Operating system (also called 'Platform'). Ideally, the software will work on an operating system that you are already familiar with or have already installed. Some applications may require a specialised database, and this poses similar issues. If you have to go beyond your existing platform, will there be training and installation issues?

Hardware requirements. You may be able to run the software on your existing servers and network, or you may need upgrades. If new equipment is required, make sure you factor it into the cost.

Licence cost. Don't forget to look at the cost, and to consider how it compares to other packages on the market.

There are several ways to evaluate packages. The best way is to see the software in action. Ideally, visit another company that is using the exact software you plan to use and see it in operation. You can then quiz the users and administrators of the system. It also gives you a chance to go hands-on with the system in order to understand it better.

Next best is to assess the software at your leisure in your own premises, with sample data supplied by the software provider. Most software companies now provide demos that can be accessed online or downloaded. However, it may take some time and expertise to actually set up one of these packages, and this needs to be factored into your planning.

You could evaluate the software just by reading the user documentation. This will give you a good idea of the functionality of the program, but it will give you very little sense of the quality of the software and how it might actually fit into your business. Unless you are quite comfortable with the software producer, and are used to the software acquisition process, don't assess software on the basis of documentation *alone*. Nevertheless, this may be a useful step to narrow your shortlist of packages to be fully evaluated.

The very worst option is to assess the software on the basis of marketing materials and the pitch of the salesperson. It's crucial that you see and use the actual software at the very least; if at all possible, you should evaluate it according to set criteria and compare it to other packages and options.

Tailor an existing package to your needs

It may be possible to tailor an existing package to your needs, or have the software company that produced it change it for you. This is likely to suit you if the package meets some of your needs but there are specific aspects where you require changes.

An example of tailoring software is to set up a link between two different pieces of software. For example, you might want to have orders go directly from a shopping cart package into your accounting software. It's unlikely that either piece of software will have the facility to do this automatically. You will need to engage a developer to build the missing link between the two.

Generally, the best people to advise on this are the vendors of the software that you want to integrate. They may be able to suggest developers and tools able to do the integration you need.

Developing a solution from scratch

Developing software tailored to your needs (also called 'bespoke software') is the most risky way to meet your Web-development requirements. Nonetheless, it may be your only option if you have very specific needs. If you are trying to pioneer a new way of doing business or to have a system that is a radical improvement over the ones your competitors have, this may be the only option.

Don't take on this option lightly. It will take a lot of work to get an application that you are happy with, and it may take quite a bit of trial and error and testing to build something that is really satisfactory. Even after you finish the main development, you will have to keep in touch with the developer to make sure that you can get updates and changes made as necessary in the future.

The following suggestions may help guide your bespoke development:

- make sure the developer (the person writing the actual computer program) has an understanding of your needs and can make contact with the relevant people as necessary to clarify any questions that arise. A well-written requirements specification and vision statement are all the more important in this situation.
- it's critical that you develop some form of prototype before doing the full development.
- don't try to incorporate too many features into the first version of the program. It is better to develop something quick and get it working as soon as possible. You can make modifications later.

Prototyping

No matter what approach to development you take, it's a good idea for the project sponsor and the project steering committee to see one or more prototypes of the system before going ahead with a full implementation. A prototype allows everyone involved to see what is actually planned, which gives them a much clearer idea than detailed specification documents. It also gives the people involved in developing the system a more concrete grasp of what the requirements are. Some large companies which spend many millions per year on IT systems are prepared to invest as much as 3% of the expected project budget in developing a prototype or proof-of-concept, even though they know that the prototype itself is likely to be thrown away.

The type of prototype will depend on the circumstances. For packaged software, it may be simple enough to set up a demo version of the software as the various software packages available are evaluated. If the software is being custom-developed for you, it may help to build some mock-up screens. Although the system developed may not be functionally complete, it will show the basic underlying concepts. This will also help flush out issues with the use cases, thereby helping all the parties involved to have a better understanding of what needs to be developed.

It's essential that the prototyped system broadly meets the vision statement set down at the outset of the project, and that it meets the requirements which were developed. You can modify the vision statement and the requirements if necessary, but this should only be done after careful consideration.

One thing to avoid is to go headlong into coding or implementing the full system. Spending some time developing specifications and prototypes beforehand will help all the parties to fully understand what is proposed.

Software and hardware architecture

You will need to determine what software platform to use. In many cases this will be easy; you will simply use whatever you or your hosting company is currently using. For a large project, or where software is only available for one platform, some important decisions will have to be made. Determining the most appropriate platform will depend on the skills available, how scalable the system needs to be, and what the budget is expected to be. It's important that everyone understands the implications of the decisions that are being made at this stage.

Coding and setup

Writing the code or plugging in the software that makes up the system is the most obvious part of the software development process, but it's not necessarily the part that takes the longest. The success of this phase will depend on whether the decisions and analysis done to date have been completed correctly.

Testing

Testing is the critical business of making sure that the software actually does what was required of it at the outset. At a minimum, it's important to make sure that all of the required use cases are taken into account. However, a modern testing process should do far more than that. Automated tests should be able to detect coding errors that are not immediately obvious. Fixing the 'bugs' or mistakes in coding that are thrown up by the testing may take as long as, or longer than, the time spent actually writing the code.

The best coding practices now require that testing goes on throughout the development process, and doesn't just take place at the end. This helps to increase quality and reduce the possibility of nasty surprises towards the end of the project.

Documentation

Software needs to be documented, and the documentation needs to cater for a number of different audiences.

Users. Users need documentation that will explain to them how to use the system. This may be included in separate manuals or help files, or it may be incorporated into the software itself.

Developers. You will need developer documentation if you develop software from scratch, or if you tailor software to your needs. At some stage in the future, you will want to extend the software system. Quite likely, the developers working on it now will not be involved in these future projects, and new developers will be dependent on whatever notes the original development team left behind. If there is no documentation, it may be difficult to understand how the system works, and this will mean that the future development work will take longer and cost more.

Implementation

Once the system has been developed and tested to a satisfactory standard, it's time to roll it out to all the various actors involved. They may need to be retrained in the new system, or at the very least informed of the changes that are being made. In many cases, new software will result in a change in work practices. This needs to be considered and managed.

Maintenance

Software development is an ongoing process. There are always changes and updates to be made, however small. To support this process, you have to make sure that a small team is kept familiar with how your software works.

The iterative process

In the processes described above, not all these steps necessarily happen only in that order. In practice, many of the steps are repeated a number of times during the development. For example, a first release of the software may have only the basic features, and the whole process is followed through again to produce a new version with extra features. Iterating in this way is generally a healthy sign, because it makes it more likely that the software is constantly reviewed and development is kept in line with requirements.

5 MAKE YOUR BUSINESS MORE EFFICIENT WITH THE INTERNET

A well-run business is like a well-designed car. It operates reliably and quickly, and with a minimum of friction, waste and unwanted by-products. It can be maintained with a minimum of hassle. Engine designers pore over plans and constantly scour the reference books for new materials and technologies so that they can make the next generation of engines even more efficient and straightforward to maintain than the previous one.

As a result, engines in motor vehicles are many times more efficient, and cars, even budget models, are far more comfortable today than they were 20 years ago. In addition, the engines are far easier to maintain, with fewer moving parts and less to go wrong.

Increasing efficiency and using new techniques is not just for car designers. As the owner or manager of a small business, you are like the chief designer. It's your responsibility not only to keep the business running smoothly, but also to constantly redesign it, so as to minimise friction and waste, serving the customer better while keeping costs low.

The Internet is the new technology that can revolutionise the efficiency and capability of your business. Just as car engineers seek out new materials and techniques to streamline their designs, you can find ways to make your business more efficient without having to compromise on quality or customer service.

Some of the changes you can make are obvious. You can use the Internet to reduce communication and purchasing overheads by going online or by using e-mail to avoid the costs of postage and couriers.

But the real opportunities come from making changes to the processes of your business so that you can cut overheads while maintaining, or even increasing, the level of service.

Let's look at two major household brands, Ryanair and Amazon, to understand how they have taken advantage of the Internet. Although these are now large companies employing hundreds of people, both companies have only grown to their current size in the last 10 years or so. They illustrate how the Internet can change a business, and even a whole sector.

Ryanair

Ryanair is a famous example of a company that has used the Internet to become more efficient and radically reduce its operating costs. Although Ryanair is now a massive company reaching into every corner of Europe, it really is a small business at heart. Only 15 years ago it was one of the smallest airlines in Europe. It still has a small, compact head-office operation and, like many small businesses, it continues to be dominated by the vision and personality of one person, the chief executive Michael O'Leary.

The company strives for efficiency and reduced costs, and this happens on many levels. On the simplest level, the company is ruthless about driving down overhead costs. The chief executive instructs his executives to collect pens and other stationery when they are staying in hotels on business trips. Not only does this save on the cost of pens, it also makes executives think about costs and how they can be reduced.

But Ryanair's efficiency derives from a lot more than saving on incidentals or driving hard bargains with suppliers. Its current success is the result of asking the following hard questions, and it has received some surprising answers.

- **Does an airline really need travel agents as its sales force?** Ryanair pays no commissions and almost all bookings come through its website.
- **Does it really take a lot of administration to run an airline?** Despite being one of Europe's biggest airlines, the administrative functions are carried out by fewer than 100 people.
- **Are customers prepared to pay more for extras like food, drinks and priority boarding?** Ryanair found that the expense of providing these services could be passed on to the customer as extra charges, which some of them would be happy to pay.
- **Should hold luggage be free?** Luggage handling is an expensive overhead for the airlines and by charging for it, Ryanair is able to take some control of the burden and the costs.
- **Is customer service and comfort really critical?** Ryanair almost prides itself on providing a low level of customer service. Customers know what to expect, and for the most part accept it.

To read more about Ryanair's background, see 'Is this any way to run an airline?', *Newsweek*, 28 September 2004 (http://www.newsweek.com/2004/10/03/is-this-any-way-to-run-an-airline.html#)

Ryanair's internal processes are radically simpler than their competitors'. It does not employ the same complex check-in systems that other airlines use, depending on simple paper-based systems rather than complex software and unreliable printers. An online content management system is used to handle a lot of the bureaucracy of manuals and notices to pilots and air staff that are essential for flight safety. There are no meals on the plane other than paid-for snacks, no division between classes, and there are no free flights or upgrades for regular customers. Ryanair focuses on airports where they can turn the plane around quickly and maximise the number of hours that they are in the air.

This hasn't been done in isolation. Ryanair has a very different relationship with its customers, compared to most other airlines. Customers deal with the airline mainly over the Web, booking their own flight by credit card and checking themselves in before they leave for the airport. No commission is paid to travel agents. Passengers know that they cannot expect a high level of service when they get to the airport. They accept that they will have to queue to get a good seat on the plane. They know they will have to pay for any refreshments. They also expect the airline's PR and advertising to be controversial.

Equally, the airline has changed its relationship with its employees. As with customers, it does its best to deal with its employees directly, and bypasses trade unions wherever possible. Computerised systems are used to dispatch rosters and other essential documentation to its staff, once again cutting down on administration.

As a result of this strategy of cost- and service-cutting, Ryanair is able to operate services on routes that would be marginal or unprofitable for other operators. This has facilitated rapid growth of the business, because the company is in a position to build new routes to destinations that would not be viable for other airlines.

The company's rapid growth has also put it in a position of strength with regard to its suppliers. It can get the best deals on new aircraft from Boeing and Airbus (it was the only airline in the world to order significant numbers of planes in the year after 9/11).

In turn, whole economic sectors have boomed on the back of flight connections offered by Ryanair. These new flights have opened up new areas of Europe to tourists. With cheap scheduled flights available, consumers are no longer so dependent on charter companies to arrange an economic trip to a far-off destination. All these changes have helped Ryanair's profitability by locking in increased regular trade, and Ryanair has become an important feature of the local economy in many places.

Amazon.com

Similarly, Amazon.com has succeeded in using the Internet to change the way that books are sold. Jeff Bezos, the founder of the company, asked the following questions:

- **Do you always need to have a shop to sell books to the general public?**

- Do you need to have every book in stock in order to be able to display it and sell it?
- Why should a small company limit itself to serving a small geographical market?

Rather than building up a warehouse of books, Amazon.com took an order for any book in print, and then sourced it from a network of suppliers. In some cases, the book could even be 'drop shipped' directly from the printer or publisher to the end-customer. Because of the well-developed system of couriers and postage in the US, this small start-up was able to service customers anywhere on that continent.

Amazon.com became not just a bookshop on the Internet, or a bookstore that was highly efficient; it was completely different from anything that had gone before. As a result, it was able to operate on a completely different cost base compared to the old-style bookstore.

At the heart, Amazon.com radically changed the relationship between the bookseller and customer, while maintaining a high level of customer service and contact. Rather than just depending on consumers to buy books, Amazon also got them to contribute reviews. The information about customers' interests is also used to drive Amazon's recommendation engine, which suggests books that might be of interest to customers, based on the buying patterns of previous customers. Additionally, it set up affiliate schemes, which paid a commission to websites that linked to books on the Amazon.com website if the link resulted in sales. In this way, Amazon.com became part of the network economy.

Its processes were radically different from any other bookseller, and allowed for its operations to be highly centralised and cost-controlled. This centralised structure enabled Amazon to quickly adapt to trends in the marketplace. As with Ryanair, rapid growth put the company in a strong position to deal with its suppliers.

It also returned to its roots – its customers – to open new opportunities. It has been able to expand into selling many other types of goods, including CDs, DVDs and consumer electronics.

Small businesses

Of course, what Amazon has done is not necessarily a guide for smaller businesses. Amazon.com's systems are the result of major investment, and its sheer scale and buying power account for a lot of its profitability. And only a company with a really strong brand can take the risk of diversifying into completely new areas.

However, small companies can also take advantage of the Internet. One example of a much smaller operator in the book business is the author Kate Thompson. Thompson had written a number of successful novels that were published by Bantam in the UK. Thompson and Bantam eventually parted company after a long relationship. Although Thompson could have sought out another publisher, she decided to see if she could find another way to sell her work to her wide global readership. She already had a popular website, and she wanted to build on this success.

She was also aware that, as a small business, she could operate much more efficiently than a large publishing house. Whereas publishers can only afford to pay a commission of less than 10% to the author after all the overheads are taken care of, Thompson could expect to receive a much higher return for each copy sold if she sold her writing directly to her readers, even though she might sell a much smaller quantity compared to selling through publishers and bookstores. Controlling her own business would also give her the ability to dictate the quality of the product.

Putting up a manuscript on the Internet would be easy enough. But how would she get readers to pay for it? Most importantly, how would she grow her community of readers and encourage more people to read her work? After all, she could no longer depend on a publisher or a global network of book distributors to promote her.

The solution that Thompson and her husband came up with was simple. She divided her new book into two sections and put the first part online, but the second part was only available for customers who were prepared to pay. To maximise sales, the book was divided after the 25th chapter, which was a real cliffhanger. Anyone who had enjoyed the first part of the book would be interested in paying for the final seven chapters.

Thompson now sells the final seven chapters, called 'The Clandestine Chapters' through her website, using the simple 'Buy Now' purchasing mechanism that Paypal provides (see Chapter 2). The Clandestine Chapters costs 15 euros, including postage and packaging, and is hand-bound with hand-made paper. The author will make an inscription with a personal message if requested. Direct communication with the author is part of the whole package, and the website carries frequent feedback from readers.

By being clever, Thompson has found a new way to market her product and brand. She is no longer dependent on the traditional distribution channels. Because her cost base is so much lower, she can operate her business in a very different way from the big players in the publishing market.

A practical guide

We can't all be Jeff Bezos of Amazon or Michael O'Leary of Ryanair. However, most companies can benefit from using the Internet to restructure their business. Some of the following techniques will help you understand how the Internet is going to impact on your industry and how it can be used to improve your business.

Stage 1: Understand your business

Before we go into the details of how a small business might use the Internet to improve efficiency, think about the following areas:

Purchasing and working with suppliers

What suppliers do you work with, and how do you communicate with them? How do you choose new suppliers? What are the critical issues for you in deciding whether to retain a supplier?

Marketing, sales and customers

Can you describe your typical customer? How does your business typically interact with them? What are the processes for ordering, dealing with complaints or returns and for dealing with post-sales issues that arise? What are the types of problems you have (if any) with customer relations? Why do some customers stay with you, while others leave to do business with someone else?

Research and development

How do you find out about new products and developments in your industry? How do you research them and make decisions about what new products or services you will offer? How do you communicate these changes to the other people in your business?

Managing information

How do you manage all the information your business generates? Do you use computer systems to do this, or do you rely largely on paper-based systems? If you use a computer, what sorts of software do you use?

The business environment

What is happening in your business environment? Are you under pressure to reduce your prices or pay your suppliers more? What are your competitors (large and small) doing that is different from what you are doing?

The financials

What is the most profitable part of your business? Where do you expect the growth areas to be? What are the biggest cost areas of your business? How does your business compare to others in the market?

Stage 2: Identifying opportunities for improvement

Once you've thought about and documented some of your processes at a high level, it's time to think about the way you could improve the service. This will vary according to the nature of your business.

Relating to your customers

Here are some ways in which the Internet could be used to improve your relationship with your customers.

1. **It can provide a new way for you to acquire new customers. Think how can you promote your business better on the Internet, and how a website might help convince potential customers to consider your company when looking for goods or services.**
2. **It can help you keep in touch with your existing customers. Sending out a newsletter through e-mail, or**

just dropping a line to regular customers might be an effective way to keep in touch.

3. It can aid the sales process. Think about whether this process can be streamlined by providing information online. Ryanair's online booking facility makes it easy for customers to find out whether there are any flights available and allows them to find the right flight at the right price. It also cuts out the middleman, thereby reducing costs.

   Amazon.com's recommendation engine and readers' reviews make it easier for customers to find relevant books than if they were in a real bookshop.

   Even if you are primarily a bricks-and-mortar business that makes face-to-face sales, you would benefit significantly if you could reduce the number of sales calls you have to make by even 10 or 20 percent.

4. It can provide post-sales support for your customers. You may be able to provide a reference section on your site to help customers with frequent questions about your product, or to provide downloadable versions of product manuals. Even a small reduction in the number of calls you receive could result in big savings. If you receive a lot of queries over the phone about the status of orders, you could reduce your costs by allowing customers to view the status of their orders online.

   Finding a way to get more direct information about your customers' needs will allow you to be more sensitive to their requirements and to react more quickly. For example, some heating oil companies now offer a facility whereby the oil supplier monitors the level of a customer's heating oil, and a delivery is automatically dispatched when supplies are running low. As a result, the oil company is able to build a more long-term relationship with the customer rather than having to put in a fresh quotation every time a potential customer rings up to ask for a delivery of fuel and having to provide a rush delivery if the tank is empty.

The same approach can be used for providing many other types of materials and is broadly known as 'vendor managed inventory'.

5. You can carry out billing and payment online. Your customers may be willing to accept invoices sent by e-mail or through other electronic systems. You can also receive payment through electronic funds transfer, thereby reducing the amount of paper involved in the payments process.

Many suppliers of accounting software now provide an 'e-business' solution that can easily be added on to your existing accounting packages. For example, Sage offers 'Sage Transaction e-Mail'. These products may provide a convenient way to automate your processes. Before you put such a system into full production, however, take the following steps.

- Make sure beforehand that the invoices it produces are acceptable to at least some of your important trading partners. If not, the system will not be of much benefit.
- Ensure the system is easy to use and that everyone involved has received the training they need to use

it. You need to be confident that the system is as foolproof as possible before you launch it.

- After you start using the system, perform regular manual checks to make sure that invoices and payments are going through smoothly.

6. You can renegotiate prices based on improved Internet-based processes. If you can use the Internet to service your customers more efficiently, you may need to renegotiate the prices you charge them. Customers who predominantly deal online should be able to take advantage of better prices than customers who are serviced by conventional methods.

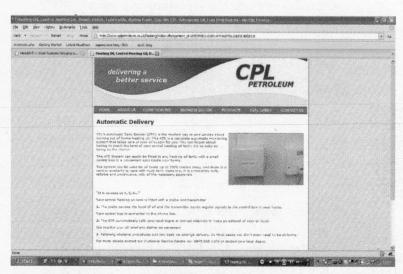

CPL Petroleum, a heating oil supplier, can monitor its customers' fuel use and can schedule a top-up delivery if necessary.

Relating with suppliers and partners

You can use to the Internet to change the way you communicate with your suppliers.

1. Searching for products and services

Do you use the Internet to search for better prices or new products? The Internet may be a good source for finding alternative sources of specialised services or commodity products. For products, look on Alibaba.com or, for smaller quantities, on eBay. Price will be just one of your criteria when purchasing. Consider, also, whether new suppliers can provide better products, better customer service or more efficient ordering systems.

Buying on eBay

No matter how good a deal you have with your supplier, there is probably someone out there on the Internet who can offer the same thing for less money. Almost any product imaginable can be found for sale on eBay, and often at a significant discount to the mainstream price. Check out the price of the tools and raw materials you use in your business to see if you can get a better deal on the Internet.

However, there are some pitfalls. A better price does not always mean a better deal. There are numerous reasons why eBay merchants can offer such good deals, so factor these in when you make your purchase.

■ The goods may be second-hand. Obviously, you cannot compare a new price from your current supplier to a second-hand price from the Internet. However, the quality of second-hand goods may be good enough to meet your particular requirements.

- The goods may have been designed for a different marketplace. Sometimes the products you buy on eBay are 'grey' goods, meaning that they have been purchased at a cheaper price in another market where these goods are less expensive or where there is oversupply. This product may be made to slightly different specifications to the one available locally. Again, this may not be a problem for you. It could be as simple as the product having a different plug, or there may be significantly different configurations. However, there may be problems sourcing spare parts, and local companies may be reluctant to provide service.

- The seller may provide a much lower level of service than you would expect from a local dealer. This is not always the case, but you cannot realistically expect the same level of service if you are paying much lower prices.

- The goods may be unbranded. The unbranded goods you find on eBay may be just as good as the big-name originals, but you or your customers may prefer to have the assurance of a well-known name.

- The seller may not be as reliable as you had hoped or your order may take longer to be shipped than expected. If possible, try to build long-term relationships with sellers you find to be reliable.

MAKE YOUR BUSINESS MORE EFFICIENT

- The shipping may cost more than you expected. Make sure you take this cost into account when you are sourcing goods from abroad. Depending on the type of goods, it can easily add 20 or 30% to the price.

2. Improving your purchasing processes

Check whether your suppliers can provide you with online ordering and payment systems. If they can, you should take advantage of this as much as possible in order to reduce the paperwork in your business.

When you start out, get your supplier to accept orders by e-mail. Even this simple change should result in improvements in efficiency over sending a fax or calling the order out over the phone. This has important advantages aside from the savings on the cost of the fax or phone call. There is far less chance that your order will be accidentally mis-keyed by your supplier, leading to you getting the wrong goods. You will also have a permanent record of the order in your e-mail software for later reference.

3. Accessing customer service

The Internet is a good way to interact with your suppliers to get customer service. If you have access to an online support database, you may be able to find the answer to your query more rapidly than if you have to wait to speak to the appropriate person on the telephone. You will also have a written copy of your query, which you can refer to later. If there is an online support forum, you can benefit from the experience of other customers in order to find the solution to your problem.

4. Negotiating a better deal

See whether you can negotiate a better deal with your existing suppliers by committing to work with them online. Some suppliers may be willing to offer a discount or offer more favourable pricing, although they may expect you to commit to a minimum volume of business as well.

Your internal systems

The Internet offers many opportunities to improve efficiency and cut down overheads within your business.

Eliminating overheads

A lot of business overheads can be eliminated by using the Internet and creating a paperless office. Obvious candidates for cutting costs are courier and postal bills, stationery bills and so on.

There are many ways to save money, but not all of them may work for you. Some savings are likely to be short term and ultimately counterproductive. Avoiding pitfalls is as important as identifying potential cost savings.

Reducing communications costs

If you can reduce your use of mail and couriers by moving over to e-mail or electronic file transfer, you will save a considerable amount of money. This should be enough in itself to justify the amount you spend on getting a good-quality broadband connection.

All sorts of documents that are currently sent by post can now be sent by e-mail, providing the other party is willing to accept them in this format. For example, invoices and statements can be converted into PDF format and sent as an e-mail attachment.

You can send any digital file over the Internet. However, some files are too large to send as an attachment to e-mail. In this case, you will need to set up an upload site to store your documentation. Your Internet service provider may be able to supply this service (ask about establishing an FTP, or file transfer protocol, site), or you can use an online service. For example, sendthisfile.com (**www.sendthisfile.com**) provides such a facility. Once you have set up a free account, you can upload any large file, and a link will be sent by e-mail to the recipient you specify. When the recipient clicks on the link, they will get access to your file. This site also offers paid-for accounts with extra features to regular users.

There will still be occasions when you need to send regular mail. Your lawyer will be more comfortable if you sign legal contracts by hand and then send them by post or by courier, although in principle, a contract entered into by e-mail should be considered as being binding. For very large files (larger than a gigabyte), it may still be more convenient to 'burn' a CD and send it by post.

Internet phone calls

You can also use your broadband connection for telephone calls. A program called Skype has revolutionised telephone calling over the Internet for individuals and small businesses.

You download and install Skype for free from the Skype website (**www.skype.com**). It will work on most computers running Windows 2000, Windows XP, Windows Vista or Mac OS X. You will need a headset incorporating headphones and a microphone to make the best use of the program, and you can purchase this online from Skype, from eBay, or from any electronics store. Once you have set it up, you will be able to talk to any other Skype user for free. The sound quality of calls is often far better than an ordinary telephone line. You can also set up 'SkypeOut', which allows you to make telephone calls to ordinary phone numbers. The cost of these calls is very low, typically around one pence per minute to call a landline anywhere in Europe or North America. If you make a lot of international phone calls, you can make big savings this way.

If you have a video camera attached to your computer (you can buy one for around £30 or less), you can also make video calls. The video is not very high quality and often lags behind the sound, but it is good enough to experiment with.

You can also make audio conference calls over Skype, with up to five different parties participating in the same conversation. Some of the participants can be Skype users, and some can be called into the conference over the regular telephone.

Although Skype generally offers good voice quality, calls do sometimes get cut off mysteriously, and you may have problems if your Internet connection is congested. So, until you are fully confident in Skype, you may want to continue to use the regular phone for calls to your customers.

Substituting regular phone calls with Skype calls should considerably decrease your monthly bills.

Alternatives to Skype

Skype is great for a small company or for use by one or two people – it's cheap and easy to use and install. But as your needs grow, Skype may not meet your requirements so well.

There are other ways to make phone calls over the Internet. In particular, there is a standard for Internet phone calls called VoIP (Voice over Internet Protocol). The benefit of VoIP is that it is an open standard, which means that VoIP phones are widely available, and these phones can be used independent of a computer. VoIP systems also have features that a company is likely to require, such as the ability to transfer calls between extensions. As your business expands, a VoIP phone system may be more useful than Skype.

VoIP services are available from a number of different companies. Some of the main companies providing the service in the UK and Ireland are:

- Blueface: **www.blueface.ie**
- Voipfone: **www.voipfone.co.uk**
- Vonage: **www.vonage.co.uk**

Outsourcing

If you are operating in a high-cost economy, you are likely to want to try and find ways in which you could get your products manufactured or get some part of your service rendered in a less-expensive location. You may discover that your larger competitors have already done this, making it hard for you to compete. It's easier for large companies to outsource, because they have the time and money to spend on finding the right outsourcing partner.

The Internet can make it cost-effective to outsource on a small scale. It enables you to get in touch with potential partners and find out what they have to offer.

If a lot of the work you do is done on computer (for example, writing reports, doing research, writing or testing computer programs or producing drawings), you can exchange files with your partner very easily. You can test out the relationship with some non-critical work to see if the arrangement is going to be satisfactory.

Outsourcing the production of a physical product is far more complex. Both you and your partner will have to invest time and money to determine the exact requirements and to make sure all the arrangements are in place so that you get the quality and service you require.

Exchanging e-mails and speaking by phone is no substitute for face-to-face meetings. Do not underestimate the importance of meeting and getting to know your outsourcing partner. Once the initial introductions have been made and samples of the work required have been passed back and forth, it's important to cement the relationship with meetings at your premises and the premises of the partner. Ongoing face-to-face contact needs to be part of the outsourcing agreement, as well as e-mail and phone conversations.

Improving organisation of information

Information is a more and more important part of every business, big or small. Even a small business has hundreds or thousands of pieces of information to keep track of. There is information about all your customers, suppliers and employees to consider. You may have a lot of documentation about the products you sell.

As the Internet becomes a bigger part of business, the amount of information will continue to mushroom. Take care not to drown in the onslaught, and put in place systems which will allow you to quickly get at the information you want.

There are many approaches to dealing with your information management.

- **Paper system.** You probably have a paper filing system in place already, and you are likely to continue to need it for some time to come.
- **Financial accounts system.** If you still keep your accounts on paper, consider using a computer-based system. It will greatly reduce the amount of manual work involved and make it easier to do your filing.
- **Contacts database.** A database of customers and prospects should be at the core of your marketing and sales efforts. It will allow you to keep track of your activities in relation to every single one. Contacts database applications are sometimes called 'customer relationship management' tools (CRM) or

'sales force automation'. Although the level of sophistication may vary, the basic idea is still the same. Some applications also provide project management or order management functions, and integrate with your accounts system.

■ **Collaboration tools.** Some companies develop a private website, often called an 'intranet site', which they use to collaborate internally within the company, and to work with partners. This has the benefit of making all the project information instantly available to all the people involved, including lists of tasks and deadlines. It also provides a useful central repository to store files relevant to a particular project.

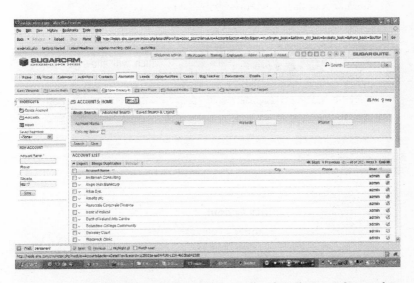

SugarCRM (www.sugarcrm.com) is one application that can be used to manage your customer and supplier lists. It is Web-based, and there is a free version with basic features that you can test out on the SugarCRM site, or get your Web developer to install for you. Other similar applications include Salesforce.com (http://salesforce.com).

There are many tools that fit into this category, and you need to choose the one that is correct for you. Some of them, such as ActiveCollab or Basecamp (see image below) provide a structured environment, and are useful for specific purposes such as planning and managing a project. Others, such as MediaWiki (the tool which is used as the basis for the online encyclopedia Wikipedia, see **www.mediawiki.org**) or SocialText (**www. socialtext.com**) provide a much more open structure, which could be used to set up a very broad knowledge base for your company.

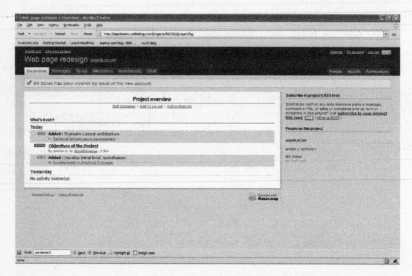

Basecamp by 37signals (www.37signals.com) provides an easy-to-use environment for online collaboration. You can try it out for free. Another similar tool is ActiveCollab (http://activecollab.com) and a trial version is available, although you may need to ask your Web developer to install it for you.

The mobile Internet

Mobile phones have become an important part of how people access the Internet. Increasingly, handheld devices, rather than computers, will be the way most people get online. As well as allowing you to browse the web, these phones allow you to download and install programs called 'apps' to add new features to your phone. This has critical implications for small business from a number of perspectives.

1. Opportunity for greater efficiency through e-mail and online applications

For a small one- or two-person company, being able to access e-mail and the web through a phone is a major boon. It is no longer necessary to be in the office, at the computer in order to deal with e-mail queries. Many e-mails can be dealt with from home or on the road. What's more, you can keep in touch with employees much more easily. They can give updates from the sites they are working on, and if they run into difficulties, they can send photographs back to the office or to colleagues to help explain the problems and to seek solutions.

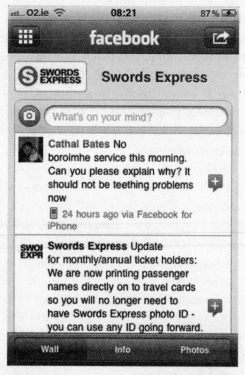

The Facebook page of Swords Express, a public transport company in Dublin, as it appears in the Facebook mobile phone app.

2. Location-based applications

We are beginning to see Internet search and web pages that are 'location aware', that is, they know where you are currently located and can suggest nearby businesses that are relevant to the user. At the simplest level, this can function as an electronic map which might allow you to quickly locate a nearby petrol station so that you can fuel up, for example. However, the potential is much greater than that. Your phone could tell you which nearby restaurants have free seats on a busy Saturday night or tell you about a good deal on tickets for a musical that is opening nearby.

Location-based mobile phone applications are really only in their infancy. Foursquare (www.foursquare.com) allows members to keep track of where their friends are and make reports on shops, cafes and other locations they visit, which are then accessible to other Foursquare users. Facebook offers a similar, though less developed facility on its mobile app. If your business is travel or tourism related,

Starbucks are experimenting with using Foursquare to offer special deals to customers who visit its stores regularly.

or depends on attracting customers off the street, then you should keep an eye on these mobile applications as they develop and as they offer more facilities for small local businesses to promote themselves.

Research and development

To find new ways to increase efficiency, be constantly on the look-out for trends in your sector and in the wider business environment. The Internet provides the perfect facility to do this, without you having to go on expensive trips or engage outside expertise.

When you search on the Internet, don't just confine yourself to finding out about products that you are already familiar with and trying to get them at a better price; look for new products and new ways of doing business. There are developments in other countries and in other sectors that will ultimately have an impact on your market and your business. Try to figure out ways to keep abreast of these changes.

This is how Michael O'Leary originally forged his plan to turn Ryanair into Europe's biggest budget airline. Although he did not have the benefit of the Internet at that stage, he carefully researched what was happening in the US aviation business and modelled his company on Southwest, a budget airline based in Dallas, Texas.

A great way to start is through a well-organised search on Google to find overseas companies that are in the same sector as your own. Their websites will provide lots of information about what is going on in their respective countries. You can discover what new products are emerging and how popular they are.

Try also to find a discussion board or a mailing list that covers your area of business, or that is frequented by customers or potential customers. By reading what is being said, it will give you clues about what is happening next, and what trends are emerging.

When you search for information about what is going on in other countries, try to understand what level of maturity that market has reached. This will allow you to compare that marketplace to your own. Typical ways of gauging the maturity of a particular market are as follows:

- **Are there a lot of operators in the market with new entrants becoming involved, or is it consolidated with a few big players?**
- **Are the most modern products being offered?**
- **Is the pricing competitive compared to your market at home?**
- **Is after-sales service an important part of what is offered?**

Remember, don't just look the products and services that are offered, but look at the whole dynamics of the industry – whether it is growing and competitive, or quite static. It's also a good idea to research countries where the Internet is making an impact on your industry. You may be able to find ways of doing business that are relevant for your market.

Look beyond your own sector to related ones that are relevant to what your business is doing. Find out how other industries are coping with the problems that you face.

Stage 3: Bringing it all together

There are hundreds of ways you can use the Internet to improve the way you manage your overheads, the ways you communicate, the ways you purchase and the ways you sell.

However, the most important thing is to see how all these changes might fit together to improve your business overall. This will give you the best clues about what your priorities should be for making changes.

Improving discrete areas of your company is important, but consider how the Internet can be used to improve the linkages between the different areas. For example, an improved system for dealing with information about customers can make your production more responsive and efficient as well as improving the performance of your sales force.

Implementing the outcomes of your research and development should result in benefits for your sales as well as for your production systems. A good choice of systems that makes the linkages between the different areas of your business much smoother, resulting in reduced overheads, is perhaps most important for a small business. The improvements you implement should result in enhanced performance across all areas of your company; for example, systems which allow better, cheaper sharing of information often bring the biggest benefits. As you prioritise the changes you're planning to make, think in terms of the *whole* business, not just one department.

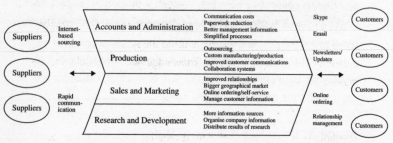

This diagram shows how the various improvements you might make to your company can fit together. This will give you a clearer idea of the biggest opportunities for change. (It is based loosely on Michael Porter's value chain model, adapted to reflect the needs of the modern, customer-oriented company.)

Stage 4: Implementing change

Coming up with possible ways in which the Internet can be used to improve your business without costing very much money is all well and good, but implementing what seems like quite a simple change can take longer than expected and have hidden costs.

Here are some tips on avoiding the most common problems.

Have a plan

Before you implement any changes, however small, draw up a plan with a clear description of the objectives, the stages and the milestones.

Keep everyone informed and listen to people

It's imperative that everyone involved (which in a small company usually means all employees) knows what is going to be changed, and why the changes are needed. The sooner the changes are signalled, the easier it will be to allay any fears that people may have. Take particular care when putting in place changes that affect people who are not yet comfortable with the technology, and ones that are likely to have an impact on people's jobs.

If you have to choose a technology platform or approach, it makes sense to get the people who will be using the system involved in the decision. Their experience and knowledge will be invaluable in making the right choice.

Understand and test the technology thoroughly

Technology is not always reliable. It requires a significant amount of testing, and you need to be quite sure that any system you want to purchase is reliable before you begin to depend on it in your business. If important information is going to be stored in a new system, it's vital that you have a procedure for making a backup copy of any data.

Refer back to Chapter 4 for further advice on the steps to take when developing or buying a major new piece of software for your business.

Have a pilot project

Rather than changing over everything in the company at once, it makes sense to test it on a smaller scale beforehand. If you are considering using a project collaboration system, test it out on one project before you try to roll it out to all the computers. Before your company adopts a desktop program such as Skype, get one or two people to test it out thoroughly first.

Check that the correct equipment and software is available

Make sure that everyone in the company has the equipment and software they need to be part of the changes. Simple things such as checking that machines are up to date, that the network connections are working and that the required software will work on all your computers are essential. Don't take anything for granted.

Have a training plan

It takes time for people to learn how to use a new system properly. Make sure that everyone involved has the correct training. Even though money may be tight, it could be beneficial in the long run to send some staff on an external training course.

Make sure you have the technical and organisational support you need

Many of the suggestions in this chapter, and in the rest of the book, can be carried out with relatively little outlay of cash, and many of the programs mentioned can be downloaded for free from the

Internet and installed either by you or by your Web developer. However, the low initial costs can be deceptive. Make sure that you have sufficient support to help you deal with any problems you might encounter as you install a new system. If you or a member of your staff is sufficiently technically inclined, then you may be able to manage with your internal resources. However, do not hesitate to get a support contract or the aid of an outside expert if it will help make your project a success.

Stage 5: Review the improvements and make further changes

The business environment is constantly changing. New software and technologies are becoming available, and something you'd like to be able to do, that is not possible at the moment, might be more workable in a year or two.

Also, as time goes on, your customer profile will change. Your customers may not be interested in doing business online at present, but in a few years, they may be more familiar with the Internet and be more willing to change.

At the same time, new players will almost certainly enter your marketplace. These will be relying on technology to give them an edge and you will need to have a strategy to deal with that.

Do take time to review regularly both your internal systems and your relationships with suppliers and customers to make sure that your business operates like a well-designed engine. There are always new technologies and new challenges to consider, and to remain successful, you have to keep one step ahead.

6 STRATEGIES FOR A SMALL BUSINESS ON THE INTERNET

Business is like judo. You have to turn your disadvantages as a small company into advantages that will allow you to succeed and prosper. As a small company, you don't have the power of scale and the ability to dominate a market that a large company has. You don't have a big budget to spend on advertising and marketing. Your product development budget is always going to be limited. You don't have offices all over the world to sell your product. You don't have the resources to build a big technical infrastructure.

However, as a small business, you do have many assets that bigger companies don't possess – such as speed, flexibility and a lack of bureaucratic hurdles – so capitalise on these and use them to your competitive advantage.

Your business has a human scale

Small businesses have one big advantage over their giant counterparts – everyone in the company knows one another. It's important for all employees, including the boss, to be familiar with the customers, their needs and their value to the company. When a customer rings or e-mails a company, he or she should be able to deal right away with a member of staff who knows something about their business.

Contrast this with the big companies you deal with. They are often impersonal, with personnel frequently being switched around. It's hard to figure out who is in charge and you may have to speak to a number of people in order to get anything done.

In some companies it can be difficult to even get to speak to the same person a second time when you telephone them. They are commonly divided into 'silos', areas of the business that do not engage with one another, and which are only faintly aware of the customers' needs.

Not all big companies are like this. The best large companies communicate well with their customers; they make sure that every customer is treated as an individual and with respect. Nevertheless, these companies have struggled hard to keep themselves focused on the ordinary customer.

Think about how you can convey this strength on the Internet. You can do it through the content on your site and through your blog. You can also do it through your e-mail and other contacts with customers.

Have a conversation with your customers

As the owner of a small business, tap into the power of the Internet to magnify your company's 'human' voice and carry it to a wider audience. For example:

■ **Use Facebook and Twitter to engage with customers. You can get instant feedback about plans and changes to your product or service. However, you should not expect your Facebook and Twitter followers to necessarily be typical of your customers generally.**

221

- use an e-mail newsletter to stay in touch with your customers on a regular basis, to keep them informed about your company and how it's growing and the new products and services it's offering
- you can use e-mail to converse directly with customers, without having to find the time to go out and meet them
- write a blog to keep in touch with the rest of your industry and with people who are particularly interested in what your company offers
- monitor and, if appropriate, participate in online forums to find out what customers think; get ideas on how to improve your service and present and defend your company's point of view

Big businesses find it hard to do these things. Decisions and public statements often have to go through so many layers of management that they are often out of date by the time they are published. Companies are petrified of taking a view on anything, for fear they will alienate some part of their customer base. Small companies can bypass a lot of these problems.

Swords Express
Travel/Leisure · Swords, Dublin ·   ✎ Edit info

Wall
- Hidden posts
- Info
- Photos
- Discussions
- Reviews
- Notes
- Edit

About   ✎ Edit
Bus service between Swords, Co. Dublin and Dublin City Centre

305
people like this

Likes

Photoireland Festival

Eirebus

The Wright Venue

Add to my page's favourites
Subscribe via RSS
Unlike
Share

Wall   Swords Express · Top posts ▾

Share: 📋 Status 📷 Photo 🔗 Link 📹 Video 📊 Question

Write something...

Swords Express
Update for monthly/annual ticket holders: We are now printing passenger names directly on to travel cards so you will no longer need to have Swords Express photo ID – you can use any ID going forward.
559 Impressions · 1.25% feedback
16 June at 16:20 · Like · Comment

👍 Elaine Byrne likes this.

💬 View all 6 comments

Suzanne Donnelly Can i get my card updated with my name on it as my annual ticket doesnt expire until next March.
Friday at 11:44 · Like

Swords Express Hi Suzanne, existing cardholders can continue to use their active cards – we will print your name on the next card that you purchase. Let us know if there are any problems, thanks :)
Friday at 15:44 · Like

Write a comment...

Sarah Kelleher
Haven't seen the drivers from the old service in ages, what happened them all?
📱 15 June at 08:50 via iPhone · Like · Comment

👍 3 people like this.

Write a comment...

Cathal Bates
No boroimhe service this morning. Can you please explain why? It should not be teething problems now
📱 12 hours ago via iPhone · Like · Comment

Swords Express
Swords Express update: we will be operating the Sunday schedule this Bank Holiday Monday, 6th June

Swords Express, a bus service in Dublin, uses its Facebook page to engage directly with customers about route changes and service problems.

MAKING AN IMPACT ONLINE

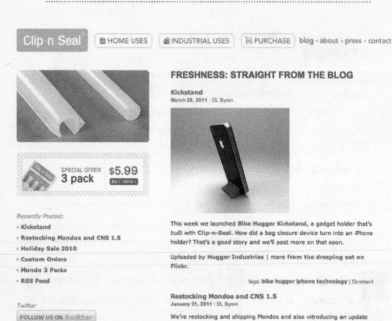

Clip·n·Seal | 🏠 HOME USES | 🏭 INDUSTRIAL USES | 🛒 PURCHASE | blog · about · press · contact

SPECIAL OFFER
3 pack **$5.99** BUY NOW

FRESHNESS: STRAIGHT FROM THE BLOG

Kickstand
March 28, 2011 : DL Byron

This week we launched Bike Hugger Kickstand, a gadget holder that's built with Clip-n-Seal. How did a bag closure device turn into an iPhone holder? That's a good story and we'll post more on that soon.

Uploaded by Hugger Industries | more from the dreeping set on Flickr.

tags: bike hugger iphone technology | Comment

Recently Posted:
- Kickstand
- **Restocking Mondos and CNS 1.5**
- Holiday Sale 2010
- **Custom Orders**
- Mondo 3 Packs
- RSS Feed

Restocking Mondos and CNS 1.5
January 31, 2011 : DL Byron

We're restocking and shipping Mondos and also introducing an update with a hollow rod this week.

tags: 2.0 cns 1.5 | Comment

Twitter
FOLLOW US ON twitter

Holiday Sale 2010
November 28, 2010 : DL Byron

All of our Clip-n-Seals on Amazon.com are on sale now through the end of the year. 20% off.

Continue reading Holiday Sale 2010

tags: amazon sale | Comment

Facebook

Clip-n-Seal on Facebook
👍 Like

34 people like Clip-n-Seal.

Michael Nick Brian Aaron
Betsy Kitty Tsuyoshi Chris

Facebook social plugin

Custom Orders
July 21, 2010 : DL Byron

We get asked this frequently and worked to simplify the process to make custom orders. We can run custom orders in our factory at any length, size, and diameter. The minimum cost to initiate a project is $3,000.00.

The small company behind Clip-n-seal mixes stories about how its customers are using its products with news about company vacations (www.clip-n-seal.com).

224

*You can listen to your customers and change
direction quickly to offer new products and services*

Speaking with a 'human' voice and having a 'human' scale for
dealing with your customers enables you to have relationships with
your customers and to listen to good ideas and then try them out.
Use the feedback you get from blogs, discussion groups, e-mail and
your sales force to find out what your customers need. Experiment
by offering new products or services, or delivering them in a
new way.

Your large competitors find it hard to do this. They have
procedures and systems to follow through when they launch a new
product, and so what might take you a week or less to achieve
could take them months, or even years. As a small company you can
quickly tap into new opportunities. You can even set up a whole
new business, with its own domain name and website, relatively
easily and quickly.

*You can benefit from the personal touch and the
personal recommendation*

As a small company with a human touch, you can benefit from
personal recommendations from customers whom you know and
who trust you. Your customers should be your most important
ambassadors. They can tell other customers what they think about
your product and what its advantages are.

As well as having an e-mail newsletter and a blog, as mentioned
above, participate in an online discussion forum, where your
comments can be helpful to and appreciated by other customers.
This will be a recommendation in itself.

Make sure the company maintains personal contact with
your most important customers. It's essential to have a system to
track these relationships. If your company is small enough, you

can do this with a carefully managed pile of business cards. If your needs are larger, you might need a CRM system (see Chapter 5).

You can build networks with like-minded companies

Don't let the fact that you are a small company limit your scope. You can work with other companies (large and small) to provide what your customers need. You won't have all the expertise in-house, but you also avoid all the associated overheads. In addition, you have the comfort of knowing that if a particular partnership or arrangement doesn't work out, you aren't necessarily committed to it for the long term.

As a small business, you already probably work with other businesses and with independent contractors, to provide extra support when you are busy or when you need specialised skills. Rather than thinking of this as a stopgap solution to deal with a short-term problem, consider using it as a regular part of your business. It can provide you with a way to grow without needing to develop and invest in a large number of staff.

Similar arrangements can be made for manufacturers. It may not be economic for you to have a manufacturer in your home country, but you can use the Internet to find a manufacturer in a lower-cost economy who can provide what you want. If you can build a relationship with them, they might even be able to tailor their goods to your specific requirements. Sites such as Alibaba (**www.alibaba.com**) provide access to manufacturers all over the world.

Outsourcing, virtual organisations and the textile Industry

Benetton, the global clothing company, is an example of a firm that grew to worldwide proportions while remaining a relatively small and compact company atthe core. The company outsourced the majority of its activities, especially manufacturing, which was handled by external companies, and sales and distribution, which were handled by a network of licensed franchisees. The marketing and advertising for which Benetton became famous were sourced from specialised agencies. The core staff was able to concentrate their efforts on steering the strategy of the company and ensuring the quality of the products, and did not have to get involved in the day-to-day detail of making deliveries or opening new stores. At the heart of the company was a computer system, which coordinated stock levels in franchise stores and re-ordered from the manufacturers as needed.

Some commentators said that Benetton (like similar companies, including Diesel and Gant) was a 'virtual' company, because it held no stock of its own and had no manufacturing, sales or distribution facilities of its own. What it did have, however, was a strong brand and a clear strategy and coherent management systems.

As it turned out, full outsourcing was a growth strategy rather than a long-term strategy for Benetton. In recent years, as the company consolidated its position, it has acquired its own manufacturing facilities and has taken greater control of distribution andsales, opening stores under its own direct control in major cities.

Although few companies will go to the same extremes as Benetton, consider whether your small company can use some of the same techniques in order to grow rapidly. Working with other companies and concentrating on your own niche (whether that be strategy and marketing, manufacture, distribution or sales) may be a way to maximise the impact you can make in the marketplace and improve profitability.

While there are many potential benefits to partnering and outsourcing, there are also serious pitfalls that you should be aware of.

- **Successful business with partners and suppliers over long distances depend on good personal relationships. Keep in constant contact with the people who manufacture for you so that you're completely up to speed on availability and quality issues. Using e-mail, Skype and other means to do this will be critical to the success of your working relationship.**
- **Structure the relationship carefully to make sure that you get out of it what you want. For example, if quality is your primary concern, emphasise this to your partners and clearly indicate in your contract the**

penalties that will be incurred if quality standards aren't met.

You and your partners have to be comfortable with the technology involved. You may need to have particular computer programs in place and have to change your procedures so that you can work together efficiently.

You can take a position and have a strong point of view in the marketplace

For the most part, large companies often don't have the luxury of taking a strong point of view and asserting it clearly and forcefully. They often seem to give out mixed messages which are hard for customers to understand. The reason they do this is because they find themselves having to cater to many different constituencies – shareholders, lenders, employees, unions and customers – and they may consider it more important not to offend someone than to have a clear message and to articulate it well.

A small business can avoid that problem. While it is important to treat all the people you deal with respectfully, you have to be able to take a position on an issue and stick to it.

Taking a particular stance about your product or your industry (for example, believing that prices in your sector are too high, or that customers deserve a higher level of service) should not mean that you stick to that, come what may. It's a starting position for your ongoing discussion with customers, suppliers and competitors. You may find that your position is the correct one for you, or you may have to adjust or soften it.

Use the Internet to express your view. You can make it known on your website, through a blog and through online discussion boards.

MAKING AN IMPACT ONLINE

You can be a member of a community without dominating it or trying to control it

As companies merge, get bigger and start to get more market share, they begin to dominate the marketplace or the community

The PGS Plumbers' Blog is run by a plumbing firm in London, and provides plenty of background information about the plumbing trade. The site incorporates video and includes links to Facebook pages and to Twitter.

in which they operate. Rather than working with the other players, or working to serve their customers better, they try to outdo the other players, acquiring them or eliminating them. They do this because they are under relentless pressure from their financial backers to succeed. Sometimes the strategy backfires, and the race to get market share may be at the cost of profitability, reputation, or worst of all, the customers' confidence in the whole sector.

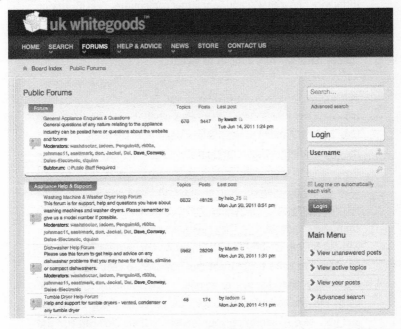

The UK White Goods forum is a place where the UK home appliance industry congregates and discusses shared issues. There are also forums that are open to consumers. A small company can benefit from the expertise of its peers through networks like this.

You are a small player in your market – you have no need to dominate it or to try and set the agenda. Although you may have a particular philosophy about your product or service, you don't need to dominate the marketplace with that point of view. Potential customers may agree or disagree, but at least they will have a sense of your company as a group of human beings who are working to develop the marketplace, rather than as a money-making machine.

You can use your Internet strategy and presence to make the difference between you and your larger competitors clear. By having a strong, visible, personality on your website and in discussion boards, your company can distinguish itself in a way that larger counterparts will find difficult to match.

Your organisation is nimble

Big companies have clear advantages when it comes to their cost base and their ability to get the best deals from suppliers. However, they have complex organisational structures that have built up over the years and these can be difficult to restructure in order to deal with changing markets and to make the best use of the latest technology. Small companies can adapt quickly to deal with changing circumstances. They can make rapid changes of direction without having to consult with numerous committees. You have to be primed to make the most of this, however, so keep up with new technology and changes or trends in your industry. Use online blogs and discussion forums to track the concerns of your customers and find ways of improving your services to them. You can also use these blogs and forums to find out about new products that are being developed. Finally, your internal processes have to be flexible and you should constantly be trying to find new ways to update and simplify them.

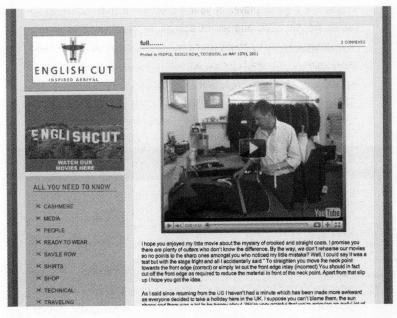

full......
Posted in PEOPLE, SAVILE ROW, TECHNICAL on MAY 10TH, 2011

2 COMMENTS

ENGLISH CUT
INSPIRED ARRIVAL

ENGLISHCUT
WATCH OUR
MOVIES HERE

ALL YOU NEED TO KNOW

✕ CASHMERE
✕ MEDIA
✕ PEOPLE
✕ READY TO WEAR
✕ SAVILE ROW
✕ SHIRTS
✕ SHOP
✕ TECHNICAL
✕ TRAVELING

I hope you enjoyed my little movie about the mystery of crooked and straight coats. I promise you there are plenty of cutters who don't know the difference. By the way, we don't rehearse our movies so no points to the sharp ones amongst you who noticed my little mistake? Well, I could say it was a test but with the stage fright and all I accidentally said " To straighten you move the neck point towards the front edge (correct) or simply let out the front edge inlay (incorrect) You should in fact cut off the front edge as required to reduce the material in front of the neck point. Apart from that slip up I hope you got the idea.

As I said since returning from the US I haven't had a minute which has been made more awkward as everyone decided to take a holiday here in the UK. I suppose you can't blame them, the sun shone and there was a lot to be happy about. We're very grateful that we're enjoying an awful lot of

English Cut (www.englishcut.com), a traditional UK-based tailor, is a company that has transformed itself as a result of customer demand through its website. Previously, the company was focused on a small group of UK customers. Through its well-written and interesting website, it has attracted many new customers in the US. Although still based in Britain, it has made changes to focus on these new customers.

Your size means you can also be flexible and fast-moving in adopting new technology. As we've seen, Ryanair is a famous example of how to use the Web to improve processes and cut costs.

The airline business is full of industry norms and accepted practices that are not really efficient and which could be radically improved by new technology. However, many airlines find it difficult to change their systems and procedures.

Ryanair has broken that mould by using the Internet to introduce a 'check-n-go' service whereby passengers bypass the check-in counter completely and proceed directly to their gate when they reach the airport. The advantage to the passenger is a more convenient journey. The advantage for Ryanair is that fewer staff are needed at the check-in desks. Although other airlines now allow

Ryanair's online check-in system. As the system is more widely adopted, it will mean that fewer check-in desks and staff will be needed, and the result will be shorter queues.

check-in over the Internet, Ryanair was the first to promote it for mass-market customers.

Why did Ryanair get there first? Quite simply because Ryanair was ready and willing to change the way it did business in order to embrace the technology fully. Bigger and more established airlines saw the opportunity but did not have the flexibility to make the necessary changes.

Many businesses can use a similar approach to Ryanair's, albeit on a smaller scale. Allowing customers to check product availability and make their own orders online can speed up production and reduce administrative costs.

Conclusion: You serve your market, rather than expecting your market to serve you

Customers are more powerful than ever before. They have Google and the other search engines to find what they are looking for. They have community sites to share experiences. It's essential to be able to respond to their needs, whether they require greater efficiency, better service or lower prices.

Technology is changing the marketplace. It offers an opportunity to become far more efficient and more customer-focused. The revolution is still taking place and there is room for imaginative small operators to do things that the bigger players haven't thought of or don't have the ability to cope with.

The businesses that will thrive are the ones that can mould themselves around the needs of customers. If you can provide the service that customers need and, in doing so, make a profit, it doesn't matter whether your business is big or small.

CONCLUSION: IT'S TIME FOR SMALL BUSINESSES TO THINK BIG

> To succeed online, you don't need massive offices, an army of staff and a bottomless pit of cash. On the Internet, a company is defined by its website and what people are saying about it.

Technology is giving small, nimble businesses an opportunity to become far more efficient and more customer-focused than ever before. The revolution is still taking place and there is room for imaginative small operators to do things that the bigger players haven't thought of or don't have the ability to cope with yet. The businesses that will thrive are the ones that can mould themselves around the needs of customers.

As a result of the same technology, customers are increasingly powerful. They have Google and the other search engines to find what they are looking for and they also have community sites to share experiences. They no longer need to stick with the same old suppliers if they can get better prices or better service elsewhere, and they won't hang about for sentiment's sake. Attracting these customers is about communicating well and providing value for money: it's not about big marketing budgets or fancy computer programs.

236

To be efficient and customer focused doesn't necessarily require very much money, although it does require hard thinking and lots of hard work. You can work with partners to provide sophisticated services and you can source products from all over the world from the comfort of your desk. You don't have to be a big company and you don't need deep pockets: you can make an impact on a shoestring and this book gives you the directions to get you started on your way. Good luck!

INDEX